Hope for lost sheep

Rejoice
with me

Annie Heppenstall

Augsburg Books
MINNEAPOLIS

REJOICE WITH ME
Hope for lost sheep

Cover image: © iStock 2020: Cheeps enjoy life in the field of countryside
Taiwan by fongleon356
Cover design: Emily Drake

Print ISBN: 978-1-5064-6020-8

For my son, Luke, and my husband, Ray,
with much love.

About the author

Annie Heppenstall is a qualified teacher and has a degree in Theology and Religious Studies from Cambridge University. She has spent the last four years practising a contemplative lifestyle, giving time to her family, to her writing and other creative expressions of spirituality as well as training in spiritual direction and counselling skills. Among other things, she is a professed Franciscan Tertiary. She lives in a richly multi-faith area of the Midlands with her husband and son.

Acknowledgements

I especially want to thank Ray for all the practical, emotional and spiritual support he gives, which is invaluable and makes my writing possible. I am grateful to The Queen's Foundation for Ecumenical Theological Education in Edgbaston, which kindly provides access to such a well-stocked library, and to Daphne Cook for her time, hospitality and support. If I remember rightly, the idea for *Rejoice with Me* emerged from a conversation with her a while back. I must also thank Nikki, a friend I made nearly 25 years ago, who I mention in the introduction. Nikki, wherever you are, I haven't forgotten you!

I am also indebted to Nicki Copeland and the readers whose insight and attention to detail have helped me to bring *Rejoice with Me* to its final form. More generally, I want to thank everybody who gives me encouragement to put thoughts on paper; it means a great deal.

Note on Scripture

I have (with one exception in the conclusion) used the NSRV translation of the Bible, which gives the unspeakable and holy name of God revealed to Moses (Exodus 3:14) as LORD. This name, represented in Hebrew with four consonants YHWH (hence the name Yahweh), means something like 'I AM' – a non-gendered statement of pure existence. For ease of reading this has been rendered as 'Lord' in this book. In my own writing, I normally avoid gendered language referring to God as first Person of the Trinity.

Acknowledgements

I especially want to thank Ray for all the practical, emotional and spiritual support he gives, which is invaluable and makes my writing possible. I am grateful to The Queen's Foundation for Ecumenical Theological Education in Edgbaston, which kindly provides access to such a well-stocked library, and to Daphne Cook for her time, hospitality and support. If I remember rightly, the idea for *Rejoice with Me* emerged from a conversation with her a while back. I must also thank Nikki, a friend I made nearly 25 years ago, who I mention in the introduction. Nikki, wherever you are, I haven't forgotten you!

I am also indebted to Nicki Copeland and the readers whose insight and attention to detail have helped me to bring *Rejoice with Me* to its final form. More generally, I want to thank everybody who gives me encouragement to put thoughts on paper; it means a great deal.

Note on Scripture

I have (with one exception in the conclusion) used the NSRV translation of the Bible, which gives the unspeakable and holy name of God revealed to Moses (Exodus 3:14) as LORD. This name, represented in Hebrew with four consonants YHWH (hence the name Yahweh), means something like 'I AM' – a non-gendered statement of pure existence. For ease of reading this has been rendered as 'Lord' in this book. In my own writing, I normally avoid gendered language referring to God as first Person of the Trinity.

Contents

Introduction:
Faith, hope and love

The Lord is my shepherd, I shall not want.
He makes me lie down in green pastures;
he leads me beside still waters;
he restores my soul.
He leads me in right paths
for his name's sake.

Even though I walk through the darkest valley,
I fear no evil;
for you are with me;
your rod and your staff –
they comfort me.

You prepare a table before me
in the presence of my enemies;
you anoint my head with oil;
my cup overflows.
Surely goodness and mercy shall follow me
all the days of my life,
and I shall dwell in the house of the Lord
my whole life long.

Psalm 23

O God, you are my God

Life is often described as a journey. Psalm 23, 'The Lord is my shepherd', describes the psalmist as a trusting sheep, travelling through pleasant and difficult terrain, always in the reassuring presence of God. This image has been inspiring people to walk in faith, hope and love through the most challenging situations for a very long time.

The psalm is for all of us, yet sometimes things happen in our lives that make trust difficult. When troubles come – which they inevitably do – rather than feeling God's loving presence, we may start to doubt that love and suspect that our difficulties are signs of divine disfavour or absence. Instead of feeling safe, we experience fear, guilt, hurt and loneliness – the loneliness of a lost sheep.

But our faith assures us that God *is* Love (1 John 4:8). Jesus, knowing how frightened, confused and alone we so often feel, came to reawaken our trust and draw us back into a loving relationship with God and with one another. His work is the renewing, refreshing and restoring of souls. One of his teaching tools was a parable, which we will come back to later, of a lost sheep, which a shepherd came to look for and restore to safety, rejoicing. Like Psalm 23, this parable is for all of us, setting us back on track and giving us confidence that God our Shepherd loves us and wants us to walk in that love, whoever we are.

In 1 Corinthians 13, perhaps one of the best known passages from the Epistles, Paul talks about the primacy of love, and what love means. He says,

> Love is patient; love is kind; love is not envious or boastful or arrogant or rude. It does not insist on its own way; it is not irritable or resentful; it does not rejoice in wrongdoing, but rejoices in the truth. It bears all things, believes all things, hopes all things, endures all things. *1 Corinthians 13:4-7*

Just as we aspire to live more lovingly towards those close to us, our church communities, our neighbours, the whole

world, we also need to accept that this is how God loves us –
albeit more perfectly. It is the love Jesus showed in his life
and death. We need to know this for sure, because there are
times when it may not seem to be true. There are times when
everything seems gloomy, night falls and not even the stars
come out to light our way. At such times, it is difficult to
make sense of anything.

Choosing to believe in God's love, even in the face of
what seems like contradictory evidence and the voices of
others who believe in a cruel god or an indifferent one, is an
act of faith. It is a little like remembering the springtime in
the midst of a bitter winter or, as Hosea puts it, waiting for
dawn in the dark of night: 'his appearing is as sure as the
dawn' (Hosea 6:3).

Others will tell us we are misguided, even foolish, but this
faith in love and the return of clarity is what can give us the
strength to carry on when others might despair or resort to
unloving, destructive behaviour in order to 'survive'. It is
our hope. If we stop believing in love, then it is as though
something inside us has died. Love is the flame, the ray of
sunshine that gives us the will to live. It enriches us, while
fearful outlooks diminish us.

In the same chapter of 1 Corinthians, Paul talks about the
lack of clarity that clouds our perspective in this life, and the
importance of faith, hope and love:

> For now we see in a mirror, dimly, but then we will see
> face to face. Now I know only in part; then I will know
> fully, even as I have been fully known. And now faith,
> hope, and love abide, these three; and the greatest of
> these is love. *1 Corinthians 13:12, 13*

This passage reassures us that we do not need to get
everything right or know everything – in fact, we cannot. We

are going to make mistakes. Even Paul was prepared to say, 'I know only in part'. There is a great deal of God and of life that we cannot possibly understand – but faith gives us hope that one day all will become clear, and then we will see divine love face to face and feel that love, heart to heart. Not only that, but I believe we will see how love was always a part of our life, and that we were never lost, but always held safe – we will understand.

This does not mean we should avoid asking questions about the meaning of life and why it is often so difficult. Questioning, thinking, reasoning and probing are human gifts which are to be valued and used. 'Test everything; hold fast to what is good,' we are advised in 1 Thessalonians 5:22. But still, God's mystery is always beyond us, and there are some things we are simply not going to know in this lifetime.

As in a dry and weary land

Everybody walks their own particular path. It can help us greatly to talk about our troubles with a wise listener or to express them creatively in some way, and so be enabled to let go of them and move on into a brighter place. Writing can be one of these soul-bearing processes. I have just put a book down in which the author confesses he is writing in order to process his own thoughts. I sometimes find myself writing for the same purpose, usually in a journal. But in this book I have no wish to go back over every stumble and fall along the way; rather I want simply to offer some reflections arising from the whole experience of stumbling and falling, and of being helped back up and carrying on.

I don't mind telling you that my journey has taken me through some personal experiences which left me feeling an overbearing and unexpected sense of failure. My feeling of failure was the inverse of preceding feelings of inflated self-assurance. That largely sums up about 20 years of my life! In time, though, I got back on my feet, with help, bruised and humbled. Humility was a word I had never really thought about before.

The prophet Micah spoke about it, long ago:

He has told you, O mortal, what is good;
and what does the Lord require of you
but to do justice, and to love kindness,
and to walk humbly with your God?

Micah 6:8

Walking *humbly*. I had walked shouting, I had walked sulking, I had walked protesting, fearful, questioning, tearful, arrogant, dejected and even submissive . . . but had I ever walked humbly? Mostly, I think not.

Preachers enjoy telling us that humility is to do with humus, the layer of decaying organic matter – dead leaves and the like – which enriches our soil and nourishes new growth. It is an earthy, grass-roots place to be, the ground beneath our feet which receives our footprints. It does not deny death, but holds it and changes it, showing us the bigger picture of life cycles and mutual interdependence. From down here, there is nowhere else to fall; we start to notice the tiny things that make up life. Ants carrying seeds, spiders spinning webs, worms processing earth, dandelions and fungi sprouting through cracks . . . and these tiny things start to matter to us. Translated, we start to notice and care about the little ones around us, because somehow that's where we are too. Jesus showed how, in this earthy place, God is at home.

God is a gardener, and grows us; we are growing towards the spiritual maturity of fruit bearing. Which of us does not

13

want to bear the fruits of the Holy Spirit that we read about in Galatians 5:22, 23?

> The fruit of the Spirit is love, joy, peace, patience, kindness, generosity, faithfulness, gentleness, and self-control.

Gardening fruit trees requires pruning as well as feeding and watering. We are pruned of our anger and hate, our selfishness, our exploitative behaviours, the idolatry of our materialism and hero worship, our egotism, our desire for worldly status and success, and it hurts. This pruning, I believe, is part of the process of growing in faith, and it is ongoing.

Looking back, I feel that a large part – but not all – of what I personally experienced as difficulty was God's pruning work. I did not want to be pruned! I thought I could produce those lovely fruits by my own efforts, but it doesn't work like that. The fruit we yield from our own self-belief lacks God's life-giving Spirit. It is plastic. It might look good to the outside world, from a distance, but it is not the real thing. I can pretend to be patient up to a point, but if God has not changed my heart, then deep down the irritation and impatience will still be there, and it will come out in the end.

Yet not all of our suffering is caused by God's pruning – what droughts and floods, lightning strikes and pest attacks does a tree endure in its life? We are part of creation, and our planet home is groaning with its own developmental processes, its own cycles of change, decay and regeneration. As I was walking in woods once, I came across ants' nests at intervals along the path – metre-wide cities of tiny, busy creatures, coming and going like the traffic on our road networks. Nothing protected them from the footfall of walkers or horses. They reminded me so much of our own bustling, self-absorbed cities, so much more fragile than we care to admit.

Like ants on the forest floor, we are vulnerable in ways we sometimes forget to the natural processes of the earth and human warfare. It is painful to be reminded of our smallness and fragility. A part of us somehow feels that we who have managed to screen ourselves so effectively from nature have a right to be protected from it. But Paul tells us that creation is waiting for liberation from death, just as we are. We are part of creation, we find ourselves in the way of its own colossal writhing, and we, like all living things, are still caught up in the pain of mortality even though our hope is of freedom and redemption – not just for ourselves but for all.

> For the creation was subjected to futility, not of its own will but by the will of the one who subjected it, in hope that the creation itself will be set free from its bondage to decay and will obtain the freedom of the glory of the children of God. We know that the whole creation has been groaning in labour pains until now; and not only the creation, but we ourselves, who have the first fruits of the Spirit, groan inwardly while we wait for adoption, the redemption of our bodies. *Romans 8:20-23*

So we face God's pruning work to refine our souls, along with the blind thrashings of a tormented earth, and we feel pain. Yet we are not wholly passive. Human beings are also pain-makers. Surely God weeps, too, at the suffering that arises from our own injustice and violence, our lack of care for one another and other living things. It is easier to apportion blame to others, including to God, than to admit responsibility. It is easier to notice our own injury than to notice the injury we cause. I believe that one element of our spiritual journey is to confess responsibility, admit guilt, and so open ourselves to God's grace, which we need in order to move forward. It is by God's grace that healing begins. It is by God's grace that our hearts are changed and we shift from violence to harmlessness. Until God changes us into gentle peacemakers, we add to the world's suffering, without even realising it.

We might call this destructiveness our 'sin', our separation from what is wholesome and loving. God knows all about it and, rather than punishing us for our failures, forgives us and redeems us, not just once but over and over again. But we find this difficult to believe, we find it difficult to give and accept forgiveness, and we punish ourselves, hate ourselves for our flawed natures. We add to our own pain by refusing to believe in God's love for us and for all creation. It seems people can believe in God's control over us, God's will for us, God's knowledge of us, God's demands on us, but something stops many from believing in God's love.

It is natural to run away and hide from what is fearful. It seems to me that, deep down – *very* deep down – we are not just afraid of God's authority; we are also afraid of the depth of divine love, because an inner voice tells us that if we once surrender to it, we will be completely consumed. God, Scripture says (Deuteronomy 4:24, Hebrews 12:29), is a consuming fire. We touch on love in moments of intimacy and we know that real love demands that we put self aside. This all-engulfing love of God threatens our egoistic minds: it will swamp us, fill us, and we do not want to be full of some alien presence; we want to be full of ourselves. No wonder we run and hide if we secretly believe God's fiery love to be the annihilation of our precious identities. Yet, once we have been touched by the fire of God's love, we know in that instant that there is nothing more sweet or beautiful; it is not the eradication of our self but the fulfilment and the enlivening of our true self. Fearful, bitter, self-centred little me will indeed burn up like chaff and die, but great self, true self, God-kissed self, will soar on wings like eagles, free and joyful because our true identity is not what we are now, but what we are to become.

As we read in Luke's Gospel, Mary the mother of Jesus puts self aside, supremely and completely, and lets God in. She lives not just in the hope but the knowledge of God's indwelling love, and bears Christ for the world. She does what we struggle to do. To the outside world, pregnant Mary is a fallen woman, disgraced and at risk of complete exclusion by her community. It seems that she is broken and lost. Yet where is God in her life? God is within, not just in her mind and her heart but in her womb, in the very depth of her being, the place within her where the miracle of life can and does happen. When life suddenly becomes difficult for Mary, she does not run and hide, and God's fullness does not diminish her, but causes her to exalt. She stands looking at us from so many statues and stained-glass windows, showing us that the consuming fire of God is wholly good, as she holds her son up for us to adore. How can it be, we might ask, that someone as lowly as Mary could be so blessed? Yet perhaps it is her very humility that makes it possible.

Life and death is bigger, more mysterious, than we can grasp. As Paul said, quoted above, 'we see in a mirror, dimly,' and we 'know only in part'. Yet our faith invites us, like Mary, to accept God's love, in a world that tells us this is nonsense. Our hope invites us to keep the faith, to be a flag of compassion in a brutal world, a world in which human beings cause immeasurable suffering and destruction. In the eyes of the world, Mary is among the suffering: poor, oppressed, probably uneducated, shamefully pregnant, her grown son tortured and executed before her eyes. 'Where is God in this?' and 'Why me?' we might expect her to ask. But the mystery of where God is in her suffering is the very mystery of our faith itself.

So I have looked upon you in the sanctuary

I cannot for a minute pretend that I am any better at saying 'Yes' to God than anybody else, or that this vast, all-consuming power of love challenges me any less than it challenges anyone else. I have not been Mary; I have been an ordinary woman, feeling not Christ growing deep within but the hurt of shame, pain, loss, confusion and other very human emotions. It has mattered to me what other people think; it has mattered to me what my different circumstances have looked like in the eyes of the world. I let the world shape my reactions and I did not stand firm; I hid away, licking my wounds.

Yet, looking back, God's love *was* there in my life, deep down in my inner being; I just couldn't often find my way to it somehow.

I want to share an experience in which a seed of God's love was sowed in me. It was to lie dormant, although still alive, for many years. My hope is that it might give some encouragement to you, or prompt you to search your own memory for moments of wonder and love.

When I was 19 I spent some weeks of my summer holiday living in a spiritual community, participating in a retreat about inner healing. Nikki, a German friend of about the same age, and I decided to spend an evening together in a large, simple room with white walls, green plants and large windows, called the 'Sanctuary'. We simply sat there in candlelight, with the idea of meditating on healing love. We had no plan other than to pray and invite Christ's presence, so we prayed and then just sat still, in silence, undisturbed.

I don't know how else to describe it than to say that love like warm, liquid light flowed into the room. It was immense, almost tangible. It surrounded us, held us, poured into our hearts and lit us up from within. At first I was so wrapped up in wonder that my whole attention was absorbed by this utterly beautiful feeling of being purely and deeply loved. All was golden within. After a while, something made me remember my friend and I turned to her. Her face shone! She, too, was being touched by this presence; it was not just for me, not just in my head, but something beyond me – us – that was for both of us. Tears of awe flowed as we realised that our sharing confirmed that this was *real*. I do not know how long we sat in this light – time somehow melted. It was very late when we finally stirred and stretched our legs in the flickering candlelight, the sounds around the big old house suddenly more noticeable again.

That, to me, was an experience of God's glory, God's loving presence, which some call the *Shekinah* – a Hebrew term. I especially warm to this name to describe my experience because many say that the *Shekinah* conveys a feminine quality of deep, compassionate love which is often associated with light – so appropriate for that candlelit evening. You might prefer to call it the love of Christ or the Holy Spirit. I'm not sure getting the right name matters too much, but today, when I am asked what I think of God, I recall this experience, and I say, 'God is love.'

Nikki gave me a poem the next day, which I still have, in which she used the imagery of Psalm 23 to express her sense that God would lead her gently through 'rough land', journeying towards a beautiful destination.

Your steadfast love is better than life

I don't know what happened to Nikki after that summer. I hope she has been able to walk in trust and love all her life.

The fact that I have not found the way so easy does not fill me with regret because I feel that I have so much to learn from. Until quite recently, though, I found it very difficult to shake off a sense of despondency that had taken hold – there was still a shadowy cloud, even once daylight had returned.

One day, this suddenly changed. I want to share this experience, too, because it has proved to be another pivotal spiritual experience for me to come back to and draw hope from. While my 'Sanctuary' experience might seem rather transcendental, this has a much more rooted sense of love at work in everyday life. It was a call back into the community of humanity and a reminder that this, too, is where God is to be found.

In 1 John 4:19-21, we read:

> We love because he first loved us. Those who say, 'I love God', and hate their brothers or sisters, are liars; for those who do not love a brother or sister whom they have seen, cannot love God whom they have not seen. The commandment we have from him is this: those who love God must love their brothers and sisters also.

Learning to love one another is part of the journey, a lifetime's work, and it can be difficult to do when we are walking alone. The Good Shepherd does not just draw us back into relationship with himself, but also with the flock, and there is no end to the challenges the flock will present to us. The work of learning to love one another is never done.

In my journal, I wrote:

> On the bus this morning, I found myself reflecting deeply on the whole of my life as though in a story or a film . . . I found myself saying, 'Well no *wonder* that happened . . .' and 'of *course* he said that . . .'

understanding myself and others as complex and interconnected characters in a slowly unfolding drama.

At last I was able to have compassion on myself, as I might have towards someone I care about. I suddenly felt kindly towards the 'me' that I have been from childhood until now. I felt able to forgive myself. I felt able to love myself, simply for being who I am with my own unique experience of life. It was as though a huge build-up of debris that had been blocking a river finally dislodged and let the river run free and clear and joyful again. I felt calm, happy, free, even excited about getting on with life. I have changed.

In the same way, I found I had great compassion for the people in my past – things just happened because of the way I was and the way they were . . . Good and bad, right and wrong are not always clear cut; the issue is so often about simply trying to cope with life despite limitations of sorrow, confusion, bitterness, hurt . . . Most of the time we are trying our best to keep a grip; some of us do so with more integrity than others, but we are striving, we are striving and God knows this.

I looked around at the people on the bus. I saw how each of these people has their own story too, their own part in the great drama, and each one is in God's hands just as I am. They are all striving, they all need so much compassion. The loved ones of people living in this city are spread wide across the face of the globe. There is a network of love, of longing, of concern and fond memories. This bus is a meeting point of love that reaches out thousands of miles in all directions – Jamaica, Iran, Pakistan, India, Poland, China, Ireland . . . and here we are, travelling this little journey together with far-reaching love in our hearts, each with our own troubles, hopes and fears, hurts and joys. In that moment I saw only a network of love, and I felt sure this is somehow of God. I felt sure that God loves us so much and aches to take us all in those wide arms to comfort and heal us, like Jesus ached to take the people of Jerusalem under his care.

Why the wait? Why the delay? Why the suffering? I don't know. But I do know that God's love is real, among and within us, now.

This was a blessing today. I felt touched by God. It was like a blind being lifted on a window, giving sudden clarity – but not given by me, I had not planned to meditate on my life and the importance of compassion on the bus. It just welled up in me, as a gift.

After this experience, I moved from feeling rather like a lost sheep to feeling like a found sheep. While before I knew I *ought* to feel grateful, happy, forgiving and trusting, I still had an uneasy sense of mistrust that would not go away. Although life seemed to be going much better, I was never sure what lay around the corner. More failure? More pain? Although I knew it was high time I let go of a lot of hurts, memories still haunted me. There was weariness and anxiety in the uncertainty. During that bus ride, it seemed as though the heavy burden fell away. It felt as though I was being given a gift, the gift of being able to forgive and love myself, and through this to forgive and love others, too. Rest assured, I don't claim to have lived in this heightened state of grace from that point on, but I now have a memory of a different way of seeing, an insight into a state of joy worth striving for. I would like to spend more time feeling like I did on that bus.

So I will bless you as long as I live

Faith or no faith, when we are troubled and messed up inside, it is very difficult to stop the mess oozing out and messing up everything outside us too. It's a vicious circle, because then we slip in the mess and down we go again. We need help, but we also need to be willing to accept help and able to recognise it if and when it comes.

In this book, I want to offer some hope and some reflections that have come out of my experience of that rough land. Whether our path is rocky or smooth, the way we respond depends a lot on whether we feel loved or not. Love is often what defines our sense of meaning and purpose, and its absence is desolation. Walking a rough path when we feel distanced from God's love is a grim ordeal, and a situation in which many of us find ourselves but perhaps don't like to admit. My belief is that God, who is love, longs for us to walk willingly in the divine presence – and also, paradoxically, with the divine presence in *us* – rather than to deny it or run away. Why, after all, would we want to hide from love?

> O God, you are my God, I seek you,
> my soul thirsts for you;
> my flesh faints for you,
> as in a dry and weary land where there is no water.
> So I have looked upon you in the sanctuary,
> beholding your power and glory.
> Because your steadfast love is better than life,
> my lips will praise you.
> So I will bless you as long as I live;
> I will lift up my hands and call on your name.

Psalm 63:1-4

ONE

Trying to hide

I have gone astray like a lost sheep;
seek out your servant,
for I do not forget your commandments.

Psalm 119:176

Where love is

Leo Tolstoy is most famous for writing the extremely lengthy *War and Peace*, but he also wrote a very short story, *Where Love Is There God Is Also*. It is a story about a Russian shoemaker who has had many unhappy experiences in his long life, which have made him an unhappy person. Then somebody tells him to start living for God instead of himself, and to read the New Testament. He is so entranced by the love of Christ that he becomes a kinder, gentler person, with more time for people than before.

One night, after sitting up late reading the Scriptures, he hears a voice telling him to look out on the street the next day because he will be visited by God. So he watches, and while he waits, he is kind to poor, cold passers-by. To everyone he meets he talks gently about Jesus and his teachings, and he also meets their physical needs. At the end of the day, he hears the voice again, speaking the words from Matthew 25:35: 'For I was hungry and you gave me food, I was thirsty and you gave me something to drink, I was a stranger and you welcomed me,' and he understands that he had indeed been in the presence of God.

When the shoemaker listens to the advice of his old friend to live for God instead of for himself, a shift begins, partly because of the advice, partly because of his decision to buy Scripture and read it, and partly because of the Holy Spirit which then works with his openness and willingness to change. I think God does work through people like that friend, to reach out to us, but I also think God waits for our response. Our 'Yes', our willingness, opens a door through which God comes, when invited. Our 'No', our contempt and cynicism, although often understandable, keeps the door closed because God respects our free will – even our freedom to shut God out of our lives.

Like Tolstoy's shoemaker, we can choose to believe in a God of love and live by that, waiting, seeking and hoping. In so doing we may well find our hope confirmed and our quality of life improved in unexpected ways. We will indeed experience God in our life.

Likewise, we can choose not to believe in any such thing, and again, we may well find our cynicism confirmed. This may mean we believe in no God, or we may believe in a God who is out to get us – a frightening one whom we would rather hide from than walk with. As we find in the pages of the Bible, people have been wrestling with such thoughts since history began.

Our spiritual ancestors

One of the things I love about the Bible is how full it is of human beings like us, who struggle to understand life in relationship with one another and with God. A great deal of the time, like us, they get in a mess. These people are our spiritual ancestors. Like us, many of them find themselves feeling threatened, hurt or ashamed, and their response is often to run away and hide – from human beings and from God. But there is a repeating theme in the Bible: when people go into hiding, God seeks them out, not to destroy them because of what they have done, but to bring them back into the fullness of life.

We will come back to some of these characters later, but in brief, Adam and Eve are the first: in disobedience they eat forbidden fruit, discover they are naked and hide from God in the bushes of the Garden of Eden, out of shame and fear. God, of course, knows where they are and seeks them out.

Jacob is another: he is on the run from his brother Esau because he has cheated Esau, who is furious. Jacob rests for a night, and there God visits him with a dream of angels and a promise of great blessing: 'Know that I am with you and will keep you wherever you go' (Genesis 28:15).

Also in Genesis we read of Hagar, an Egyptian slave who flees into the desert in fear of her mistress, Sarai, having become pregnant. Death seems inevitable, yet she is met by the angel of God who gives her water and hope.

Moses, brought up as a prince, flees Egypt after he has killed an Egyptian in a fit of righteous anger. He is afraid news of his act will reach the authorities so he escapes to Midian and works as a humble shepherd. There, in his place of refuge, he receives an awesome revelation of God in a burning bush. God's Holy name is revealed and God sends Moses to lead the Hebrew slaves into freedom.

Elijah the prophet is another: he runs away to the Negev desert, lies down under a broom tree and hopes to die. He is not running away from God but from his nemesis, Queen Jezebel, who wants to kill him. God's angel brings food and water to Elijah in the desert, refusing to let him give up, and sends him on the next stage of his journey, further into the desert where he has an amazing experience of God's presence (1 Kings 19).

In the New Testament, the disciples hide after Jesus' crucifixion. They are hiding from the authorities, in terror lest they too be arrested, but also in shame because they deserted Jesus in his hour of need. This must have been one of the most miserable groups of people in history. But then the risen Jesus comes into their locked room and says, 'Peace be with you.' From this transforming moment, they have new strength and a new confidence in Christ.

None of the characters' experiences of the divine are 'deserved' (with the exception perhaps of Hagar), but all are richly life changing. Jacob has been dishonest, cheating his brother of his birthright – yet God blesses him. Moses has killed someone – yet God blesses him. Elijah, too, in spiritual elation, commits an act of violence and then suffers from depression – and God blesses him. The disciples are weak, fearful, lacking understanding, disloyal – and God blesses them.

It is not that these people are being rewarded for the terrible things they have done, or that they are 'getting away with murder', sometimes quite literally, but that they are already suffering in their own hearts, and this is why they are hiding. But God knows their hearts and reaches them: through dream, through strange natural phenomena, through angels and other people, through Jesus himself. I think there is a vital message of grace for us to draw hope from: God does not give up on us, whatever we have done and whatever misfortune has happened to us, even when we are inclined to give up on God.

'Where are you?'

Like the characters in the Bible, God never stops seeking us out in order to draw us back into loving relationship, and although this relationship can be a challenge, even a path to the cross – real physical, spiritual and emotional hardship – the cross leads us on to resurrection joy. When we hide, when we run away, when we get lost, God says to us,

'Where are you?' and full of love, seeks us out, lifts us up and restores us. This, to me, is good news for all of us.

We can draw great strength from many passages in the Bible which convey God's mercy and grace. One story in particular which expresses the determined way in which God searches for us in our wilderness hiding places is the parable of the lost sheep, found in Luke.

> Which one of you, having a hundred sheep and losing one of them, does not leave the ninety-nine in the wilderness and go after the one that is lost until he finds it? When he has found it, he lays it on his shoulders and rejoices. And when he comes home, he calls together his friends and neighbours, saying to them, 'Rejoice with me, for I have found my sheep that was lost.'
> *Luke 15:4-6*

We will spend some time with this parable later on, but for now it is enough to notice how strongly the character of the shepherd is portrayed to act as the agent of change, lovingly searching and finding us. The Good Shepherd wants us to feel safe and to feel that we belong within community. The Good Shepherd shows the forgiving, friendly face of God and the universe.

Nothing can separate us

I have two tatty old bookmarks in my Bible which have been there since the early days of my conscious faith journey. One contains the words of Paul in Romans 8:38, 39:

> I am convinced that neither death, nor life, nor angels, nor rulers, nor things present, nor things to come, nor powers, nor height, nor depth, nor anything else in all creation, will be able to separate us from the love of God in Christ Jesus our Lord.

The second is a yellow, photocopied sheep on which I wrote my name. I don't think the two pieces of paper belonged to the same sermon, but over the years they have become connected in my mind. Paul, in the Romans passage, says that separation from the love of God is impossible. This is something to hold on to, because life experience can give a different impression: we can come to feel very, very far away from love. Jesus told many parables which help us think about God's love, but my sheep bookmark draws attention especially to the parable of the lost sheep, which can help us to accept the reality of divine, loving presence as something that accepts and affirms us, lifts us up and restores us when we feel lost and afraid.

It took me a long time to realise that although we may *feel* estranged from God, we are not. The problem is in our own hearts and minds, not God's. Although we may try to hide from God, or turn away, there is nowhere we can go from the divine presence, nor would we want to if we believe that presence is love. Scriptures such as Psalm 139 tell us that there is nowhere we can hide from God, and that we live in God's presence.

> O Lord, you have searched me and known me.
> You know when I sit down and when I rise up;
> you discern my thoughts from far away.
> You search out my path and my lying down,
> and are acquainted with all my ways.
> Even before a word is on my tongue,
> O Lord, you know it completely.
> You hem me in, behind and before,
> and lay your hand upon me.
> Such knowledge is too wonderful for me;
> it is so high that I cannot attain it.

Where can I go from your spirit?
Or where can I flee from your presence?

Psalm 139:1-7

God already knows. God already knows *us*. God already knows everything. How we feel about that depends on who or what we think God is. We need confidence in God's love in order to feel safe enough to come out of hiding. As with Adam and Eve hiding among the foliage of the garden, God says, 'Where are you?' not because God does not know, but as an invitation back into relationship.

Being a mother shows me something of God's love, in human terms. Before motherhood, I hadn't understood how unconditionally a parent is able to love, nor the powerful, protective, fierce nature of love that can burn so strongly it becomes comprehensible that one might be ready to give up their life for another. If a human can love this much, then how much more must God love us?

Marriage, too, shows me something of God's love. As a young person still to discover the joys and sorrows of partnership, I had no idea of the intimacy that was possible between two adults in love. I could not imagine being so close to another person as to feel that one could almost step inside them, nor the desire for that sense of knowing to go ever deeper, as love becomes ever more profound. The question is the same: if a human can love this much, how much more must God love us?

In the love we give and receive from others, there are times when we know we have been touched by something profound, something divine. As we yearn to be with our loved ones, so much more does God yearn for us, and as we treasure moments of oneness with one another, so God waits with infinite patience to be one with us. Spiritual experience is not just about the transcendent; it is also about the earthy

31

love we discover for one another. God's love is not just sublime, reserved for heaven; it is rooted, it is incarnate among and within us.

Although I often find myself talking about God, I particularly remember one conversation. I said then, as I say now, that 'God is love' (a quote from 1 John 4:8). My friend accused me of naivety, sentimentality, oversimplicity and lots of other things – in fact, he was quite cross with me. He said it was more complicated than that; he wanted God to be something – or someone – stronger. At the time, I wondered if he was right; perhaps I was being naive. Perhaps it *is* more complicated than that. But all the same, the words of the Song of Songs ring true:

> Love is strong as death,
> passion fierce as the grave.
> Its flashes are flashes of fire,
> a raging flame.
> Many waters cannot quench love,
> neither can floods drown it.
> If one offered for love
> all the wealth of one's house,
> it would be utterly scorned.
>
> *Song of Songs 8:6, 7*

If I were to have that same conversation with my friend now, my answer would be that I do not think there is anything stronger than love, no greater motivation for acts of courage and sacrifice, no greater meaning or purpose for living. The passion in our faith only blossoms as we start to discover God's love for us and our love for God, for one another and for all that God has made. If we never have a sense of that divine power, if we base our faith wholly on reasoning, or insecurity, or habit because that's what we were brought up to do, or fear of hell or hope of heaven, or belief in our own capacity to do good, then a vital ingredient is missing.

When asked what the most important commandments were, Jesus quoted passages from the Hebrew scriptures about loving:

> Jesus answered, 'The first is, "Hear, O Israel: the Lord our God, the Lord is one; you shall love the Lord your God with all your heart, and with all your soul, and with all your mind, and with all your strength." The second is this, "You shall love your neighbour as yourself." There is no other commandment greater than these.'   *Mark 12:29-31*

But how can we even begin to follow these commandments if God's love is not real to us? How can we possibly love God with all our heart, soul, mind and strength unless we are first touched by God's love for us? 'We love, because he first loved us' (1 John 4:19).

If we do not believe in God's love, other images of God are likely to dominate – judge, king, father, mother even. While all these say something about God, they do not say everything. But when love touches us, we are changed and these images melt as we realise they are not enough. Try as we might, our attempts to describe love are always inadequate; it is an inner knowing. God is lover of our souls, with a deeper and more perfect love than we can ever comprehend. That, as I suggested above, can be an unnerving thought.

The Song of Songs gives some rather enigmatic advice to a would-be lover:

I adjure you, O daughters of Jerusalem,
by the gazelles or the wild does:
do not stir up or awaken love
until it is ready!　　　*Song of Songs 2:7*

It might simply be advice to a young girl to be cautious about entering into a love affair until she is fully ready for it. Yet the girl in the Song of Songs plays the mystical part of the human soul, sought after by God, the lover. It is advice to the soul, to beware committing before she is ready. Why? Because God's power is so great it sweeps us off our feet. We have no control over God, and once the divine presence enters our lives, we do not know what will happen next. Really, we are never ready – we are always taken by surprise.

We can and should ask God to show us this love, but when we ask, God may respond in a way that is not necessarily what we would expect. We may want an immediate response yet find ourselves waiting years. We might want gentleness and feel bowled over, or want muscular intervention and receive a tickle; we might want a feast, to find we are being fed morsels, few and far between. A few years before the candlelit evening I described in the introduction, I attended a service for Christian healing ministry. I had never been to anything like this before, and not having an illness, I was not sure what to say. But when I was offered prayer, I said I wanted to know the love of God, so the minister laid his hands on me and prayed. I felt uplifted, but over the next few days I was very disappointed to find that my heart had not been opened any more than it was before. I was not glowing with a holy radiance, I was not all wise and I had not become the next Mother Teresa.

I did not get the quick response I wanted – the fast track to saintliness – but I do think my prayer began to be answered, and is still being answered, gradually, sometimes imperceptibly, but continuously. This is happening, I think, because God is continuously and unconditionally pouring out love. It is not God's limitation but mine that has caused me to be so slow to notice it and welcome it, time after time. Opening oneself, emptying oneself, even for a moment, is a welcome sign to God's in-dwelling Spirit.

I often look back to that prayer request in order to make sense of my experiences. Many of the things that have happened to me made no sense at the time, from the crushing sense of failure to the discomfort of illness and the internal struggle with self-blame and loss of self-esteem. In time, the only creative way to look at these difficult times has been to ask how I might learn from my mistakes: how to love better, how not to love, what loving my neighbour means and what it does not mean, what loving myself means and how to notice God's love. It's a never-ending lesson in love, and one I have resisted, with energy – yet I asked for it.

To conclude this chapter, let me share some beautiful words from Daniel 10:19. Being those of an angel, a messenger of God, I see in them a universal quality which seems to be for all of us, not just for Daniel, to whom they were originally spoken:

> Do not fear, greatly beloved, you are safe. Be strong and courageous!

TWO

Getting lost

How do we get lost? Why do we hide?

According to the Gospels, Jesus healed or restored people to
wholeness and full participation in the community by telling
them their sins were forgiven. We might find in this a
reflection of the words in Psalm 23:2, 3:

> He makes me lie down in green pastures;
> he leads me beside still waters;
> he restores my soul.

Within the Church, there are recognised routes for experiencing
that same grace, which involve us unburdening ourselves of
the difficult feelings which weigh us down and opening
ourselves to receive forgiveness and peace of mind. The idea
of 'restoring' is an important one. It implies the return to our
proper state, the way God wants us to be. For God surely
wants us to be in love with and to be fully open to receive
the divine love that is constantly poured out for us, and in
that love to find the meeting of all our needs and the
capacity to reach out to others in their need.

The paths to peace offered by the Church can be invaluable
for spiritual health, yet there are still times when it is very
difficult for us to believe the words of forgiveness and
healing that we hear. We convince ourselves that we are still
outside God's love, cut off, excluded, an exception to the
promise of forgiveness. When I talk in this book about
feeling 'lost', it is this feeling of being outside of God's care
that I am referring to. It is a *feeling*. I do believe that it is not
reality, because there is nowhere we can go away from God's

love; nothing can separate us from that divine love, not even our own waywardness. We can turn our back on God, as the earth in its night-time turns its back on the sun, but God is still there. We can shut our eyes, but we are still known and loved.

Lostness involves a degree of distress and/or error of judgement which leads the wanderer into trouble. Of course, not every wandering sheep or goat down in a valley or up on a mountainside is lost. A solitary figure may be quite happy and safe. Here are three clear ways of getting lost: sin, failure and wilfulness. You may want to add to the list.

1. Lostness, sin and grace

Feeling lost or separated from God is an age-old experience. Isaiah 59:2 says, 'your iniquities have been barriers between you and your God'. We might ask who builds the barrier. Is it God, to punish us by cutting us off, or ourselves because we are ashamed or afraid? I believe it is the latter.

A frequently used word for both the iniquity itself and the feeling of separation is 'sin'.

We sin easily, even naturally, and in countless ways, often even without realising. Certainly we *should* try to behave well – but it is by God's grace, not our own moral superiority, that we ever manage to do good or start to understand what is really asked of us. This is why all glory is given to God for our worthwhile moments, all humility is needed and all readiness is required to admit our imperfection, as we refuse to judge another lest we, too, be judged.

Paul says in Romans 3:23 that 'all have sinned and fall short of the glory of God'. Although there is plenty of advice in our Scriptures on trying to live a good life in harmony with other people and with God, the crux of the matter is not whether we achieve this or not. We cannot fully achieve moral perfection, try as we might. It is not about ticking off 'achievements' like the man who asks Jesus how to gain eternal life. Jesus advises him first of all to keep the ten commandments. When the man replies, 'Teacher, I have kept all these since my youth' (Mark 10:20), Jesus does not say, 'Well done'; rather he throws what seems to us and to the questioner an impossible challenge – to sell all his possessions, give the money to the poor and follow Jesus. Now I know many, many Christians who are all trying to live a good life, but the ones who have followed this last instruction are a distinct minority. Even if we were to take up the challenge, the gesture would still mean nothing without love. It is insurmountably difficult to attain God's kingdom by our own efforts. We get there by God's grace and by God – love – working in us.

Grace is a gift. We cannot rely on our own righteousness, but Scripture tells us we can rely on our faith in God's grace through Jesus. This means different things to different people, but most agree that it means 'good news for sinners' – which is all of us. Our sin, our lostness, is known and God has dealt with it, is dealing with it, and will deal with it. God does not want sin to be a barrier to relationship, and Jesus, in my view, proclaims this in his life and death.

When the risen Jesus is about to leave his disciples in the account of the ascension, he says 'that repentance and forgiveness of sins is to be proclaimed in his name to all nations, beginning from Jerusalem' (Luke 24:47). According to Luke's Gospel, this is Jesus' parting message. Jesus came to tell us about and *show* us God's mercy and grace, God's desire for relationship with us. He wanted his disciples to spread that message of good news far and wide, among the lost and the broken, the frightened, the ashamed, the wicked and the despairing. God's love is for all of these people – all of us.

The truth is, we only really appreciate what good news God's grace is when we have seen our own limitations. Until then, we continue to trust not in God but in our own righteousness. This self-righteousness is a hidden danger, because by relying on ourselves we elevate ourselves to become the god in our lives. It is by admitting our need of God that we are safe. For a person of faith, worldly failure is not the catastrophic end that we fear; it is a wake-up call to reality.

2. Worldly success and failure

Not all hiding from God is to do with guilt about moral 'sin'. Sometimes it is more to do with other kinds of failure. Secular self-help books sometimes advise visualising success, telling the reader to use positive thinking to create a greater sense of self-belief so that goals become achievable. But as long as there is a vision of success, there is also a reverse image: the nightmare of failure, which the reader must *not* focus on!

But God does not have an ego-boosting agenda for us at all. Divine interest may not lie in climbing the career ladder, or any other venture, whether we give glory to God or not. God is more interested in winning back our straying hearts and souls. We may find our plans disrupted; like the disciples we may find ourselves stripped of security, in what looks to the world like madness or misfortune. We will only begin to see the value if we look through eyes of faith, hope and love.

Many of our 'worldly' failures cause us great distress, and somehow we get muddled up and think God will despise our failure too. Self-esteem gets entangled with our spirituality. But while we might feel like hiding from the world, these are times to retreat *into* God, not away from God. Brokenness can actually lead to a deeper relationship with God. God will not reject us when we miss the mark, fail the grade, lose the contract, shoot ourselves in the foot or get rejected. God will hold us, even if we do not know it. God, who is prepared to go through crucifixion, dies with us and rises with us, too. What suffers when we fail is not our soul but our ego (I use the word in the popular sense relating to our sense of self-importance rather than the technical psychoanalytical term). When our pride shrinks, our soul can grow.

It took me a long time to realise that God is never going to massage my ego. Quite the opposite: God is taking my ego apart, bit by bit. I build it up – or let other people build it for me – and God takes it down. I am sure this is an essential aspect of the spiritual journey. It can be very painful, especially when we resist – which we do. Because 'self' is so important to us, it can feel as though God hates us – but quite the opposite is true. God is a gardener who loves us like prize vine trees. All the sprawling, straggling branches we send out, making our presence known, twisting and twining our way upwards and outwards, God clips back and trains, because this is how to cultivate the best grapes.

When the ego is dismantled, one feels empty, without pride, without ambition, without the desire for acclaim from other people, without any sense of 'wonderful me'. This may not sound like a very enjoyable state to be in, and it isn't. But from this point the restoration can begin. God does not stride in like a life coach to help build esteem and self-image right up again as it was before. God seeks to make something new, to replace confidence in self with confidence in Christ. God does this not from the outer position that the world sees, but from within. Emptied out, God can flow into us. And what do we do? We resist! We build new barriers! Feeling well again, we make our plans to 'go it alone' and rebuild our lives. As a teenager might tell a parent, we say to

God, 'I don't need you now.' But we always need God. Surrendering our will to God is a lifelong humbling process that challenges us minute by minute, hour by hour. Unless we decide to live in hope and trust God, we may not even start the process.

It seems that worldly success is not the ultimate desire or goal of a person of faith, but rather that they wish for a life lived in love with God, and thus also with others, with creation and with oneself. We cannot want this until we discover that God is love. We cannot consent to the surrender of our will until we know we are in safe hands. Until we have absolute trust, absolute confidence in this divine love, the minute we sense that we are being asked to hand over control, we run away and hide. Often we hide in our own busyness, fresh attempts to prove how capable we are. We tell ourselves we are doing good in the world and that God will be pleased with us, but really, we are back at the same game of seeking approval. Ever patient, God does not give up.

3. Running away

Another reason for feeling far from God is when we deliberately run away because God seems to be pushing us in a direction we do not want to go. The Book of Jonah gives us an illustration.

> Now the word of the Lord came to Jonah son of Amittai, saying, 'Go at once to Nineveh, that great city, and cry out against it; for their wickedness has come up before me.' But Jonah set out to flee to Tarshish from the presence of the Lord. He went down to Joppa and found a ship going to Tarshish; so he paid his fare and went on board, to go with them to Tarshish, away from the

presence of the Lord. But the Lord hurled a great wind
upon the sea, and such a mighty storm came upon the
sea that the ship threatened to break up.   *Jonah 1:1-4*

The sailors are afraid and ask Jonah what to do. He tells
them to throw him in the sea, which they do very
reluctantly. Once they do this, the storm abates. Jonah, as far
as they can see, is lost. It probably seems that way to Jonah,
too. God, however, has other ideas. As many a Sunday
school child delights to hear, 'the Lord provided a large fish
to swallow up Jonah; and Jonah was in the belly of the fish
for three days and three nights' (1:17). His journey then
continues: he finds himself going to Nineveh after all, still
arguing with God. Although it may not be pleasant in a
fish's belly, Jonah sings God's praises nevertheless.

Then Jonah prayed to the Lord his God from the belly
of the fish, saying,
'I called to the Lord out of my distress,
and he answered me;
out of the belly of Sheol I cried,
and you heard my voice.'   *Jonah 2:1, 2*

Put another way, I think Jonah is saying, 'I was lost, but you
found me.'

This brings us to the parable of the lost sheep.

The parable of the lost sheep and its relevance to this book

The parable of the lost sheep is set in a context where
'sinners' are coming to listen to Jesus. Some religious
observers take offence, so Jesus tells them about the lost
sheep and the good shepherd. The concern the shepherd

43

shows is the same that any person in the same situation would show for the animals in their care. Identifying with the lost sheep, the conditions of righteousness and unrighteousness, God's unconditional love and wilderness are all themes we will explore further. Although we looked briefly at the text of the parable in Chapter 1, here it is again:

> Now all the tax-collectors and sinners were coming near to listen to him. And the Pharisees and the scribes were grumbling and saying, 'This fellow welcomes sinners and eats with them.'
>
> So he told them this parable: 'Which one of you, having a hundred sheep and losing one of them, does not leave the ninety-nine in the wilderness and go after the one that is lost until he finds it? When he has found it, he lays it on his shoulders and rejoices. And when he comes home, he calls together his friends and neighbours, saying to them, "Rejoice with me, for I have found my sheep that was lost." Just so, I tell you, there will be more joy in heaven over one sinner who repents than over ninety-nine righteous people who need no repentance. *Luke 15:1-7*

Who is the lost sheep?

The lost sheep is equated with 'sinners', 'sin' being the first of the reasons for getting lost, which we explored above. Sin, by its definition, is not only going against God's law of love, but it is also the state of trying to separate ourselves from God – denying, hiding or running away – because of our sense of unworthiness. Scripture tells us that, like it or not, none of us is perfect, so the concept covers all of us, although we identify with the image more strongly at some times in our lives than at others.

Divine joy

This parable is the first of three in Luke's Gospel in which Jesus describes the joy of finding something or someone that was 'lost'. After the lost sheep that is found by the shepherd, we hear about a woman who finds a lost coin and then about a father who welcomes home a son who has just wasted his fortune on dissolute living. Through these parables, Jesus gives us an insight not only into our delight when we discover the kingdom or the power of God, but also into God's delight in us and God's patience and determination in seeking us out.

Righteousness and unrighteousness

The open objection of 'righteous' people to 'unrighteous' ones receiving attention from Jesus is a theme we find elsewhere in the Gospels, such as the statement in Mark 2:16, 17 after the call of Levi:

> When the scribes of the Pharisees saw that he was eating with sinners and tax-collectors, they said to his disciples, 'Why does he eat with tax-collectors and sinners?' When Jesus heard this, he said to them, 'Those who are well have no need of a physician, but those who are sick; I have come to call not the righteous but sinners.'

Jesus does not view lost sheep as a nuisance that distract him from the main purpose of guiding already godly people; rather he sees them as the key purpose of his mission. He reaches out to the lost; he makes the wilderness his lodging place.

In the wilderness

The parable of the lost sheep is located in the wilderness – that is, an uncultivated place. The Greek word is *eremos*, which can be as extreme as a barren desert or sometimes simply an expanse of meadowland on a hillside outside an area of human settlement. As we shall explore later, it is often used as a metaphor for our feelings of lostness. The shepherd leaves the flock, presumably somewhere reasonably safe, to go and search for the stray.

The wilderness has huge importance biblically, so we will give it more time and thought later, in the chapter on biblical background. For now, it is enough that the 'wilderness' is a place where we humans are not in control, and not being in control can be a disturbing experience. To be alone, like the lost sheep, rather than with companions in this 'uncivilised' place, may be doubly disturbing.

The good news

The good news is that the lost sheep is not left to its fate, is not punished or even told off, but is lifted up and brought back to safety because the good shepherd is all compassionate. We stray, yet we are still valued, and God who knows where we are will lift us up and restore us to healthy relationship, not only with God but with the rest of the flock. This does not mean we become physically immune to all further hardships of life. It does not mean we are spared rough paths and gloomy valleys from then on. It means we have a new impetus to walk in the confidence of Christ, living in love rather than cut off from love.

The promise of the parable is a promise of God's love, in which we can hope. It feeds our faith. But we know from painful experience that we can hope and hope, wait and wait, yet still feel great distress. So why do we have to wait so long? How is it that we can feel so alone for so long that we risk giving up on God completely?

I cannot answer that question, except to say that in my own life I see at least three factors that slowed me down. First, at times I resisted being lifted up because I was not convinced that those strong arms would carry me to safety.

Second, I think there was (and still is) inner work for me to do in the wilderness. There was a humbling and an emptying that I needed to endure because of the way I was. In my earlier life, I was so full of myself that there was little room for God's Spirit – yet we are meant to be God's home. I needed to be emptied out before I could be filled. I needed to see my smallness in order to begin to appreciate God's incomprehensible vastness.

Third, I was looking for God to come riding over the horizon like a knight in shining armour, while all the time I was ignoring the daisies of delight that were sprouting at my feet. I was looking for the wrong thing in the wrong place.

I don't know about your faith journey, but I believe that if we keep walking, meaning opens up to each of us in time, but not always in the way we expect. The meaning that is given to us by God is always deeper and more satisfying than the meaning we try to construct for ourselves, or the meaning the world tries to give us, but it is not without challenge and it does not preclude the setbacks and constraints that 'the world' presents to our faith path.

Sharing a personal perspective

In the parable of the lost sheep, you might find you identify more strongly with some characters than others. Personally, in my early days of faith, it is fair to say I identified most strongly with the 'righteous' people. Although they are cast as Pharisees and scribes, they are a caricature of a universal human trait. We all know people of our own faith who think they are right with God because they live according to certain principles and manage not to make a public mess of their lives. Even worse, they think this gives them the right to pass judgement on the failings of others. Sadly, I talk about 'them' when I should include myself; it is easier to spot this trait in other people than in ourselves.

As a young person, my sense of moral and spiritual superiority was strong. I was a very active Christian, involved in lots of charity work, thinking about ordination, turning up diligently to serve at the altar every Sunday, studying the Bible . . . I thought God should be really pleased with me. A sudden jolt shook me out of that sense of spiritual pride as I was confronted one day by the consequences of my own confused immaturity.

It doesn't matter what that jolt was, but its impact was that for the first time I now felt unsure where I stood with God. In fact, I felt alone; my sense of black and white, of right and wrong, had turned to grey. It was as though I had been flipped over like a coin. Heads: sure of myself; tails: uncertain of my worth, and it made me want to creep away from people who knew me. It made me unsure about my position with God. I had, almost overnight, become the lost sheep, cut off from the flock and, as it seemed, the Shepherd. This did not happen just once, but many times in my life in different ways.

Now I am able to see what I could not see at the time: evidence of God's love in action, working not to prevent but to redeem my inevitable mistakes; not to protect me from pain but accompany me through it, to bring me over and over again to a point of renewal, a new beginning; a journey from lost to found, the experience of restoration. We are encouraged to think of God as our parent, and in a way this is how a parent behaves with an older child. Hard though it is, we cannot protect our children from everything; each has to learn from experience. So we watch them, we suffer more than we let on, and (ideally), we are there for them with unconditional love when they need to come home. I am sure that the same care is God's gift to all, not because we deserve it, but because God loves us.

THREE

Biblical background

Before we go any further, it is time to turn more directly to the Bible. There are three themes to explore in this chapter.

First is the location of lostness itself: the wilderness. The Bible has a great deal to say about deserts and wilderness, and many spiritual thinkers have written in depth on this subject.

Second, there are characters from the Bible to think about who, like us, sometimes struggled to live well, and who we might see as hiding or running away from God or from God's community.

Third, we will look at sheep and shepherds in the Bible and how this imagery is used of God and of humans, whether alone or in a 'flock'.

I have included questions and suggestions for reflection. Give them as much or as little time as you like before continuing.

The wilderness

Closeness to nature

As mentioned briefly above, the Greek word usually translated as 'desert' or 'wilderness' – *eremos* – can be used to refer to a variety of habitats, some more desolate than others. It signifies a place that is outside civilisation.

Wilderness often comes up in the Gospels. Jesus and John the Baptist both spend a good deal of time there. John makes his home in the Judean desert, perhaps living in one of the many caves there, and people go out to him to be disturbed by his austerity as well as his words. He is outside the city, outside convention and culture, protection, conformity and bustle, and from this position he appears to hear God's message with great clarity, as one sees the stars more clearly in the night sky, far from city lights.

For Jesus, the Judean desert is also important, being the arena for his temptation, the place to which he is driven by the Holy Spirit after his baptism by John. But Jesus is also described a number of times in the Gospels as going deliberately into wilderness places to be alone in prayer.

Jesus, we need to remember, was a great deal more in touch with the natural world than many of us. He would walk mile upon mile through the countryside, over hills, through valleys, beside lakes and fields, watching the changing agricultural seasons, often sleeping outdoors, as he brought his message to the villagers. And his message is illustrated throughout with observations from nature, which he knows his listeners will understand. Perhaps they understood better than we do. This affinity with his environment helps us to think of Jesus as our shepherd, since a shepherd *would* be familiar with the wilderness, know how to survive, know where to find water, know how to respond to wild animals, know how to find the way, and know how to cope with the changing weather and seasons.

Jesus' parables are full of illustrations from creation and the agricultural cycles of that time and place. To appreciate many of them, we have to make a leap back to a simpler and more precarious lifestyle that was dependent on pastoralism, grain crops, olive groves and vineyards, sun and rain. Areas of human habitation were much smaller than today, and surrounded by stretches of potentially dangerous land which were the haunts of wild creatures, robbers and – as many believed – mischievous or malevolent spirits. These places had to be travelled through to get from one settlement to another, as in the story of the Good Samaritan, in which a lone traveller is attacked on the desert road between Jerusalem and Jericho (Luke 10:25-37). Often overlooked in interpretations of this parable is a fact Jesus' listeners would have spotted straight away – that he sets out alone, wearing clothes of a quality worth stealing, on a notorious road. He is unwise, to say the least.

For reflection

- You might like to pause and build up a picture or a description of Jesus in his closeness to the natural world, drawing on the Gospels, and pondering how this relates to his prayerfulness.
- Think also about your own relationship with the natural world and what it reveals to you of God.

Temptation

The short description of Jesus' temptation in Mark's Gospel makes reference to three different presences with Jesus in the wilderness during his ordeal: Satan, wild animals and angels.

> And the Spirit immediately drove him out into the wilderness. He was in the wilderness for forty days, tempted by Satan; and he was with the wild beasts; and the angels waited on him.   *Mark 1:12, 13*

Satan is a spiritual entity about whom we do not hear a great deal in the Hebrew Scriptures. In chapters 1 and 2 of the Book of Job, he obtains permission from God to test the righteous Job, and in Zechariah 3:1-5, stands ready to accuse Joshua the High Priest. He thus has an adversarial role, mischievously or malevolently set on getting humans into trouble. This is in keeping with the role he plays in the temptation of Jesus. The idea of Satan being the embodiment of all evil and an apparent threat to God's power is a later development.

We each interpret what was going on during the temptation in our own way. Was Jesus wrestling with his own conscience and identity, 'Satan' being an egoistic inner voice? Or was there an evil presence that was deliberately seeking to thwart God's work? In our own inner struggles, we might ask the same questions. Do our temptations emerge from within ourselves or from a malevolent force beyond us? Is Satan trying to stop us coming to God, or are we our own worst enemy?

However we choose to see such spiritual challenge, it is worth remembering that the Christian faith is not a dualistic battle between equally matched forces of good and evil. In Christian thinking, God, who is good, is ultimately supreme; angels and fallen angels are both created beings as are we, and operate only within the parameters allowed by God. We are taught by our faith to call on God or on the name of Jesus for help in our spiritual struggle, and to have confidence that God's goodness will prevail. The experience of wrestling with 'evil' influences is part of life, and part of taking responsibility for our own choices and behaviour. But it is one that can frighten us and dominate our outlook, and it can become a path to terrible feelings of lostness if we start to feel we are being overtaken by harmful influences – human or otherwise. At such times, we may find that God's help comes through caring people, many of whom have been through similar struggles themselves and emerged the other side.

For reflection
- What would you count as negative influences on your life, and what as positive?
- Pause for a while and reflect on what the line in the Lord's Prayer, 'Lead us not into temptation, but deliver us from evil', means to you.

Animals and angels

As well as Satan, Jesus is 'with the wild beasts; and the angels waited on him' (see above). Wild beasts are one of the risks of the wilderness, but also one of the joys. In that region at the time of Jesus, many of the bigger predators such as lions had been hunted out, but there were still wolves, poisonous snakes and biting insects as well as the gentler grazing animals and birds. Western European wilderness today is rather depopulated of creatures. If we spend a whole day in the countryside, we feel lucky if we see deer or a buzzard, partly because the creatures that *are* there are so good at hiding from us – and we rarely feel 'with' them unless we go to great lengths.

Being 'with' wild animals is not easy. So what does it say about Jesus? Are they drawn to him, as in the stories of St Francis of Assisi, over a thousand years later? Does he have that special quality of harmlessness which animals can sense? Or is this a matter of great faith in the presence of danger, as with Daniel in the lion's den (Daniel 6:10-28)?

As well as the animals, we are told that Jesus was ministered to by angels, messengers of God. The Bible contains hundreds of accounts of angels, including visitations in the desert, keeping people alive (such as Hagar and Elijah) who would otherwise perish from heat exhaustion and lack of food and water. We might ask whether these lifesavers are spiritual beings or human desert dwellers, but their presence, whatever we decide, is of God, to aid a person's survival in desperate conditions. From this we might glean hope, for in our own experiences of great need, we, too, are sometimes surprised by help from unexpected sources, which might seem very much to be divinely sent.

For reflection

- Pause to think about animals for a while. Which do you particularly like or dislike? When Jesus talks about animals he sometimes alludes to their characteristics, such as the passage where he mentions serpents, wolves, sheep and doves (Matthew 10:16). What creatures represent different qualities and feelings to you?
- What are your thoughts about angels? (The Letter to the Hebrews offers us some food for thought in chapters 1 and 2.)

Place of prayer and retreat

In Christian tradition, there are several distinct ways of looking at the desert or wilderness. One way is to see it as a place of retreat outside of everyday life. It is the opposite of town and city, a place that is not controlled by humanity. The wilderness lies beyond cultivated gardens, orchards and fields. Because of this, encounter with God who created these wild places can be very strong, direct and personal. Throughout the story of our faith, people have gone to natural deserts or wildernesses by choice to fight their inner demons, embrace simplicity and encounter their Creator through creation itself. We might find a model for this, not in the extraordinary account of the temptation, but at the beginning of Jesus' healing ministry:

> That evening, at sunset, they brought to him all who were sick or possessed with demons. And the whole city was gathered around the door. And he cured many who were sick with various diseases, and cast out many demons; and he would not permit the demons to speak, because they knew him.

> In the morning, while it was still very dark, he got
> up and went out to a deserted place, and there he
> prayed. And Simon and his companions hunted for
> him. When they found him, they said to him,
> 'Everyone is searching for you.'   *Mark 1:32-37*

This 'deserted place' is not as harsh as the Judean desert into
which Jesus was driven for his temptation; it is a grassy
hillside outside the fishing village of Capernaum. Jesus
prays alone, outdoors in natural places, away from people.
The pre-dawn retreat he makes here is a much-needed pause
following great public excitement, and before he sets out to
cause similar excitement in neighbouring villages.

There are other figures in the Bible who spend time alone
in nature. Isaac, son of Abraham and Sarah, is walking in the
fields when he sees the caravan bearing his bride-to-be,
Rebekah. The meaning of the Hebrew is unclear. Some
translations say he was just walking there – perhaps
reflecting on the way God used to walk in the Garden of
Eden with Adam and Eve, in the cool of the evening. Other
translations interpret the word to mean he was meditating.
The King James Version of the Bible, for example, says, 'And
Isaac went out to meditate in the field at the eventide'
(Genesis 24:63). We can, of course, walk and meditate or
pray at the same time.

In Judges 4:4, 5 we read of a wise leader of the people in
the time before a monarchy:

> At that time Deborah, a prophetess, wife of Lappidoth,
> was judging Israel. She used to sit under the palm of
> Deborah between Ramah and Bethel in the hill country
> of Ephraim; and the Israelites came up to her for
> judgement.

That is, she chose a shady landmark as her place to sit, located in the hilly countryside between two towns. Here, people could find her if they wanted to ask her advice. I imagine her wisdom came from long hours of prayer and reflection outdoors under the tree.

Elijah is well known for his experience of God in the silence after the storm, while taking refuge in a cave up a mountain in the Negev desert (1 Kings 19), but this was not the first time he encountered God alone in the desert. Some time before this, he warned King Ahab that a drought was on the way, then went to live in the desert fed by God:

> So he went and did according to the word of the Lord; he went and lived by the Wadi Cherith, which is east of the Jordan. The ravens brought him bread and meat in the morning, and bread and meat in the evening; and he drank from the wadi. *1 Kings 17:5, 6*

It seems that the desert is the place to which Elijah flees whenever he feels unsafe, and each time he is sustained by God.

The inner room, our wilderness

We each need our own safe, solitary space where we can be with God. One of the problems with ordinary life is that it can be very difficult to find the time and means to step out to a natural place for prayer. I think Jesus knew this, which is why he made it easier for us: he did not say, 'Do what I do – go to the wilderness and pray under the stars in the presence of wild animals and angels.' Rather, he said, 'Whenever you pray, go into your room and shut the door' (Matthew 6:6).

This closed room becomes the desert, the place of encounter with God. Voluntarily going to the room or to the deserted place is a 'Yes' to prayer, a 'Yes' to God and the

action of somebody who trusts in the divine presence. But it is as easy to face a troubled spirit here as in a real desert; physical location does not stop issues coming up that need to be addressed. Perhaps, again, Jesus' caring forethought shines out here, because our room is an easier place from which to ask for companionship and support if we do encounter difficult feelings. It sometimes helps to know there are people around.

When we are 'lost', we find excuses not to go to this place of prayer. We crowd out inner solitude and intimate prayer time with the busyness of everyday life, or even sometimes the uplift of shared worship. Why might we do this? We might be afraid of what we think God will say to us in the silence. We might doubt the presence of God and dread to discover that the silence is empty and meaningless. We might be angry or mistrustful because we are blaming our unhappiness on God. We might fear that our inner demons, real or psychological, will get the better of us – perhaps even jump into the emptiness and take us over. Such feelings are considered in the reflections that follow.

For reflection

- What is your experience of spending quiet time alone in prayer? If it is not something you normally do, consider setting a little time aside to try it, or reflect on why you choose not to.

City as desert

The wilderness will at times seem inhospitable. Our prayer times, too, can sometimes become dry and seemingly empty. But few deserts are completely devoid of life. Life exists under the surface, emerging at night and when the rains come; it finds a way to survive the harshness. Humans may struggle, but life itself is bigger than humanity. Like Elijah, we may find ourselves sustained through the driest of times in surprising ways.

Interestingly, while the city and desert have long been set in contrast, some people today see our inner cities as deserts, where life is squeezed into the tiny cracks and neglected corners. But this desert is different – it is not the desert of the Bible, where one is free of the effects of 'civilisation' to commune with God. It is a human-made environment, expressing tight control over the natural world, some might feel destructively. Where God is and how God can be experienced in such an environment are questions well worth asking. Part of the answer, I think, is to look within. Somehow, our humanity carries God's divinity into the dingiest and harshest of places, and it is often through other people that we discover the presence of God's Spirit.

For reflection
- Where is God for you, in the heart of the city?
- Take time to visit a heavily built-up area and look for signs of life. Notice the people, notice the natural resources that have been processed and used in construction, acknowledge your own feelings and be open to God's presence.

The wilderness of the exodus
We cannot talk about the wilderness without considering the Exodus, the journey of the Hebrew people from slavery in Egypt into the wilderness, where they journeyed for 40 years before reaching the 'Promised Land' of abundance in which they could finally settle. The freed Hebrews were led by Moses, whom we shall come back to below. He led God's people like a shepherd. When he reached the end of his

days, he asked God to appoint a successor to lead the people, 'so that the congregation of the Lord may not be like sheep without a shepherd' (Numbers 27:17).

The Israelites spent a whole generation in this nomadic, wandering state; not slaves, but not settled with a place to call home either. In that time, they lived in special relationship with God, who protected, guided and fed them, and moulded them into a holy people. It was a difficult time, with many hardships to endure, many challenges to their sense of trust and obedience. This was a journey which taught them to follow, taught them to trust and to wait on God. Not everybody came through the ordeal with shining colours. Not everybody followed well, or willingly, but God was always with them.

Our own journeys through life sometimes seem like an epic trek through the wilderness. We have our leaders – some better shepherds to us than others – and we have our tradition, which we are learning to understand as we go along. What is the enslavement from which we are fleeing? And what is the promised land we hope for? The walk is part of the process, the learning to trust, the discovery of what freedom and obedience mean. We have our Shepherd in Jesus, but like the Israelites of long ago, we do not always follow well or willingly.

In this wilderness walk, we are in a special relationship; this is a time to learn God's ways. While we still hope for a green-grassed future, our past is behind us; we are free to live in the moment and to walk each step in trust. The story of the Exodus helps us to accept that this walk is not as easy as it sounds. When we tire, when we argue with God, when we turn away and break faith, we are not alone. Our spiritual ancestors struggled too, but God's presence was always with them – a pillar of cloud by day and a pillar of fire by night.

61

For reflection

- What people have led you and inspired you? What are the qualities you see or saw in them that made you want to follow their lead? You might like to find out more about the lives of these inspirational figures through the internet or by reading biographies and autobiographies.

Return and restoration

Because of the way Israel's history worked out, a group of Jewish people found themselves back in the wilderness several centuries later. The kingdom which had gradually grown up and then divided eventually fell to the neighbouring 'superpower', and many inhabitants of the land were either killed or dragged north across the desert to a life of captivity in Babylon. Now the wilderness was a place of desolation which added to their suffering, and physically separated the Jews from their homes. Fifty years later, there was another power shift and the Persians, who had conquered the empire, sent the Jews back across the wilderness to rebuild Jerusalem. Interestingly, the Persian Emperor Cyrus, who decided to set the Jews free, is described in Isaiah as God's shepherd:

> [God] who says of Cyrus, 'He is my shepherd,
> and he shall carry out my purpose';
> and who says of Jerusalem, 'It shall be rebuilt.'
>
> *Isaiah 44:28*

The returning Jews are a flock of sheep, no longer exiled but travelling through the wilderness in joy. The Bible gives us images of abundant life: the wilderness, often depicted as dry and harsh, now bursts with greenery and living water:

Thus says the Lord:
In a time of favour I have answered you,
on a day of salvation I have helped you;
I have kept you and given you
as a covenant to the people,
to establish the land,
to apportion the desolate heritages;
saying to the prisoners, 'Come out',
to those who are in darkness, 'Show yourselves.'
They shall feed along the ways,
on all the bare heights shall be their pasture;
they shall not hunger or thirst,
neither scorching wind nor sun shall strike them down,
for he who has pity on them will lead them,
and by springs of water will guide them.
And I will turn all my mountains into a road,
and my highways shall be raised up.

Isaiah 49:8-11

We can see the imagery of a flock being led through once-difficult terrain that is now made pleasant through God's blessing. The biblical promise of the transformation of dry desert into lush pastureland is one of great hope that has kept faith alive for many in difficult situations through the centuries.

For reflection

- In our own times of difficulty, how can we take these words of hope to heart and let them give us hope too?
- And just as help came from an unexpected source – the Persian Emperor Cyrus as God's shepherd – how open are we to God's support and kindness expressed through those outside our own tradition?

Biblical characters

It can put things in perspective to remember that people have always gone through difficult times. The people the Bible tells us about were no less human than we are and often got into quite serious trouble. Some even ran away to hide from God, yet there is also so much hope in their stories. Sometimes we see reflections of their lives in ours. Here we will look are some key figures; we will revisit several of them later in the book.

Adam and Eve

Read Genesis 2:4–3:24.

The first couple in the Book of Genesis were also the first to hide from God. Why were they hiding? They had eaten fruit from the forbidden tree of knowledge after they had been warned not to, on pain of death.

> They heard the sound of the Lord God walking in the garden at the time of the evening breeze, and the man and his wife hid themselves from the presence of the Lord God among the trees of the garden. But the Lord God called to the man, and said to him, 'Where are you?' He said, 'I heard the sound of you in the garden, and I was afraid, because I was naked; and I hid myself.'
>
> *Genesis 3:8-10*

The man, Adam, says his fear is linked to his nakedness. The fruit has changed him and his partner Eve, and they are now aware, conscious, capable of embarrassment, uncomfortable about standing naked before God and one another. There is a fear about being fully exposed or known.

There are aspects of ourselves that we do not want others to know because they are private. There are also aspects of ourselves that we might wish God did not know about, and times in our lives when we want to do what this primal couple do – slink into the bushes and hide from God.

How do you hear the question from God, 'Where are you?' Does it sound threatening, or perhaps sad?

Although the couple have to take some responsibility for their actions, God addresses their embarrassment by providing clothing:

> And the Lord God made garments of skins for the man and for his wife, and clothed them.　　　*Genesis 3:21*

For reflection

- God's sensitivity to and covering of human shame seems to me to be an act of compassion. What do you think?
- And how do you feel about God knowing all there is to know about you?

Hagar

Read Genesis 16:1-15.

Hagar is in a deeply unhappy situation. She is a slave to Abram and Sarai who are unable to have children, and she is given by Sarai to Abram to act as a surrogate mother. Since Sarai owns Hagar, any children she has will also be Sarai's. This is not an easy situation for us to come to terms with; our twenty-first century values are so different from those of this period of ancient history. Hagar is described as showing contempt for her mistress once she is pregnant, and she is treated so harshly she runs away.

Running away, for Hagar, is a desperate act. This is a nomadic community living in tents in the wilderness, so if she leaves the protection of the settlement her life is in danger from heat and thirst, hunger, wild animals and human desert dwellers.

How does this desperation translate into modern life? Who are the ones who feel so exploited, humiliated or abused that they take such great risks just to break free? Perhaps you identify with Hagar in some way yourself.

Hagar is not running away from God; she is running away from community, the flock. Genesis 16:7, 8 tells us:

> The angel of the Lord found her by a spring of water in the wilderness, the spring on the way to Shur. And he said, 'Hagar, slave-girl of Sarai, where have you come from and where are you going?'

The angel tells her to go back to Sarai, but also talks to her about the child she is carrying and the many descendants she will have. It seems in these circumstances that going back to the community was the only way for Hagar and her baby to survive, but it must have taken courage. What she had now, though, was hope, and the memory of God's angel. In awe, she exclaims, 'Have I really seen God and remained alive after seeing him?' (Genesis 16:13).

Some years later, Hagar and her son Ishmael find themselves back in the wilderness, sent away because Sarai (now Sarah) has a child of her own – Isaac. Hagar expects them both to die, but again the angel of God comes to help her, with the message, 'Do not be afraid.' A spring of water appears and they are saved (Genesis 21:8-21).

The messages of angels often contain the reassurance, 'Do not be afraid.' This is surely because God really does not want us to be afraid, but to trust.

For reflection

- In difficult times, what thoughts and experiences have sustained you?

Jacob

Read Genesis 27:1–28:22.

Jacob is one of the twin sons of Isaac and Rebekah. Like Hagar, he runs away from people, not God – on this occasion his brother Esau, who is violently angry with Jacob for tricking him out of his birthright. Jacob heads for an uncle he has never met, far away. It seems that he never sees his mother again, and only sees his father years later after he has reconciled with his brother, as Isaac lies dying (Genesis 35:27-29).

Perhaps you have suffered family rifts, broken relationships, regrets; perhaps you have had to travel far away from loved ones, or know people in this situation.

While on the run, Jacob stops to rest for a night at 'a certain place', which he later names Bethel – 'House of God'. How must Jacob be feeling as he shelters in this place, having left his family home for an uncertain future? Yet in the night he receives comfort.

> And he dreamed that there was a ladder set up on the earth, the top of it reaching to heaven; and the angels of God were ascending and descending on it. *Genesis 28:12*

God speaks to Jacob in the dream, telling him that he will return to the land and that his many descendants will thrive. God gives a beautiful promise:

> Know that I am with you and will keep you wherever you go. *Genesis 28:15*

Jacob has not earned this promise of divine presence and protection; in fact, he has behaved quite unreasonably towards his brother, and also his father, by deceiving him. Yet God reassures Jacob, giving him strength and purpose to keep going, telling him that he will come back one day with a family.

Just as Jacob does not deserve blessing, neither do we, but all of us, from Jacob and his ancestors to our own times, are touched by this same promise of God's presence. God is with us and keeps us wherever we go. This is simply the truth: we are in God's presence wherever we go:

> Am I a God near by, says the Lord, and not a God far off? Who can hide in secret places so that I cannot see them? says the Lord. Do I not fill heaven and earth? says the Lord.   *Jeremiah 23:23, 24*

For reflection
• Looking again at the biblical quotations in this reflection on Jacob, which one speaks to you most strongly?

Moses
There is a great deal to read about Moses, but for his early life go to Exodus 1–2.

It was said of Moses in his later life, 'Now the man Moses was very humble, more so than anyone else on the face of the earth' (Numbers 12:3).

Where did he get this great humility? I wonder if it came from reflecting on his earlier experiences.

Moses, the great shepherd of the Hebrew people, is given this task by God, who speaks to him while he is in the wilderness guarding his father-in-law's sheep. God attracts Moses' attention through a bush which is on fire yet is not consumed by the flames, and reveals the divine, sacred name which is not to be uttered aloud. Awed and honoured with this unique revelation, Moses is then given the commission to go to Egypt and bring out the enslaved

Israelites. After putting up some resistance, Moses finally obeys and spends the rest of his life leading the people, with his brother Aaron and sister Miriam, on an epic journey through the wilderness towards the promised land of abundance.

What had Moses done to receive such special attention? It would appear from his earlier life that he did not deserve it at all, yet God saw qualities in him which could be put to use – perhaps the qualities he had learned as a humble shepherd.

In his earlier life, Moses was the Hebrew foster son of an Egyptian princess and grew up in court as a prince. Exodus 2:11, 12 tells us:

> One day, after Moses had grown up, he went out to his people and saw their forced labour. He saw an Egyptian beating a Hebrew, one of his kinsfolk. He looked this way and that, and seeing no one he killed the Egyptian and hid him in the sand.

When Moses realises that people know about this deed, he is afraid. Pharaoh hears of it and seeks to kill Moses, who flees through the desert to Midian. This is no small journey to make; it must have taken him a long time. In Midian beside a well, he meets his future wife – she and her sisters are shepherds – and so he joins the woman's household and becomes a shepherd (Exodus 2:16-22).

Something in this great journey through rough land changes Moses, humbles him, and turns him into the person God needs him to be. Had the story stopped at Moses' killing of the Egyptian, we might simply dismiss this angry young man and say it was no wonder Pharaoh executed him. But his life goes on, and God uses him in an amazing and unique way.

For reflection

- When do we give up on people because of what they have done? Does God give up on them?
- How does it feel to hear the suggestion that God is still with you and looks at your potential for good, no matter what? Do you accept the idea or do you struggle to accept it for some reason?

Elijah

Read 1 Kings 18:1–19:18, or the shorter account from 1 Kings 18:20.

Elijah is a fascinating character, full of passion and conviction. Sometimes what he says and does rings true even today, but sometimes he seems to go too far for our modern sensibilities. One such occasion is a strange, elemental contest between God and the Canaanite deity, Baal. Elijah triumphs, offering an apparently miraculous conflagration to God while the sacrifice on the pagan altar remains unburned. But his excitement turns to violence and he kills many priests of Baal. Not surprisingly, Queen Jezebel, who sponsors them, is furious and seeks Elijah's life. He runs away to the Negev desert, lies down under a broom tree for shade and says, 'It is enough; now, O Lord, take away my life, for I am no better than my ancestors' (1 Kings 19:4).

Reading on, Elijah starts to sound very sorry for himself, telling God that he alone is faithful. However, God seems to ignore this plaintive voice and declares that there are seven thousand in Israel who have never worshipped Baal. The self-pity does not win great sympathy.

Back under the broom bush, Elijah is visited by an angel bearing bread and water, who tells him to get up and eat. This happens twice, then Elijah is strengthened for the long journey to Horeb, the Mount of God (also known as Sinai) –

the same place where Moses saw the burning bush and then later received the Ten Commandments. Here he has a powerful mystical experience of the presence of God as a deep silence, following a raging storm, earthquake and fire.

> He said, 'Go out and stand on the mountain before the Lord, for the Lord is about to pass by.' Now there was a great wind, so strong that it was splitting mountains and breaking rocks in pieces before the Lord, but the Lord was not in the wind; and after the wind an earthquake, but the Lord was not in the earthquake; and after the earthquake a fire, but the Lord was not in the fire; and after the fire a sound of sheer silence. When Elijah heard it, he wrapped his face in his mantle and went out and stood at the entrance of the cave. Then there came a voice to him that said, 'What are you doing here, Elijah?' *1 Kings 19:11-13*

For reflection

- There are suggestions today that perhaps Elijah was bipolar or suffered some other symptoms of depression. How does this idea relate to the way we regard extremes of behaviour today?
- When have you experienced moments of calm, silence, stillness in your life?
- How might you answer the question from God: 'What are you doing here?'

Jonah

Read the Book of Jonah (it is only 4 chapters!).

Jonah is a very reluctant prophet. God wants him to tell the people of the great city of Nineveh that they must repent or face calamity. Jonah is an Israelite, and Nineveh is the capital of the Babylonian empire, so this is quite a tall order. 'Jonah set out to flee to Tarshish from the presence of the Lord' (Jonah 1:3). He gets a boat at Joppa and they set off for Tarshish – an unidentified location, possibly Tarsus in Ancient Spain. The trouble is, God's presence goes with Jonah. Like Adam and Eve, he seems to think he can hide from God – but how can one hide from God who fills heaven and earth?

The words of Psalm 139 almost seem to anticipate Jonah's plight:

> Where can I go from your spirit?
> Or where can I flee from your presence?
> If I ascend to heaven, you are there;
> if I make my bed in Sheol, you are there.
> If I take the wings of the morning
> and settle at the farthest limits of the sea,
> even there your hand shall lead me,
> and your right hand shall hold me fast.
>
> *Psalm 139:7-10*

Jonah intuits that the ensuing storm at sea is because of his presence on the boat, and he bravely tells the sailors to throw him overboard. They are reluctant to do this, not wanting the death of an innocent man on their hands, but once they obey the storm subsides. We know what happens next in the story – Jonah is swallowed by a sea creature and regurgitated on dry land, and he goes to Nineveh after all and delivers his message.

Jonah discovers that God is even with him in the belly of the 'large fish' and with him as he visits Nineveh. There is nowhere he can flee from God's presence, try as he might. This is an annoyance to Jonah.

For reflection
- How do you relate to Jonah? Is there anything in his personality that you recognise in yourself of someone you know?

The disciples
Read Mark 14:32-72 and John 20:19-29.

The disciples do not come off very well in the accounts of Jesus' arrest and death. They never really seemed to understand their teacher properly, and at this moment of crisis they display weakness, fear, misunderstanding of what is going on, and disloyalty. The women followers, it has to be said, show a great deal more backbone, loyalty and initiative – but perhaps they were not at quite so much risk of arrest and death as the 12 men.

In our world today, we are constantly faced with media images of brutality, and people in our midst have sought refuge from death threats and torture. Perhaps you yourself have suffered. So this event is not locked in the past. There is something very human in the disciples' response. With their leader dead, they hide, it seems in the same room where they shared their last supper with Jesus. But the power of that evening has gone, the body has been broken, the blood shed, but it makes no sense. Their fear is that their blood will soon be shed, too, and who wants to die for a hopeless cause?

Perhaps something in that despairing huddle of disciples relates to something in your own life.

The wonder is that Jesus knew they would behave like this. He told them, 'You will all become deserters; for it is written, "I will strike the shepherd, and the sheep will be scattered"' (Mark 14:27, quoting words from Zechariah 13:7). He told them that Peter would deny him. He knew

that Judas would betray him. After his resurrection, he goes
to them in their locked room, and what does he say? 'Peace
be with you' (John 20:19, 21).

Where is the bitterness? Where are the recriminations?
There are none. Jesus brings words of healing and
reconciliation to these troubled souls that he loves so much
and understands so well. I think those words are for us, too,
in our own weakness and despair: 'Peace be with you.'

Thomas is missing from that locked room when Jesus
appears, and refuses to believe what his friends tell him. He
insists that he must see the evidence for himself. It appears
that Jesus knows, and a week later he comes back to the
same room when Thomas is there, and again says 'Peace be
with you' (John 20:26). How patient; how gentle!

Our humanity is understood. Jesus in some ways makes
huge demands of his followers, but then at the last forgives
all. His love is so great, I think this is all he will ever do for
any of us who have tried to follow, struggled and failed. We
are no better than those disciples: we will let him down and
he will still bless us with his presence and his words of
peace.

For reflection

• What situations in your life would you like (or
would you have liked) Jesus to step into with his
message of peace? Imagine him doing just that.

Sheep and shepherds

From a twenty-first century western standpoint, it is
very difficult to imagine first-century Mediterranean Jewish
experience of Roman occupation, but it is worth a try. The
Gospels, especially, can seem so alive and relevant that it is
possible to forget they are older than the Domesday book by

a thousand years, and from a culture very different to our own. The accounts about Jesus and the early Church portray many real people, remarkably like us, but they lived in a very different world.

When Jesus told the parable of the lost sheep, what gave him the idea? What made him decide it was the best illustration of the point he was making? What was so special about shepherds? What different levels of meaning would his listeners have understood by his parable that we miss if we know nothing about sheep or Hebrew Scripture? An exploration of the Bible can help us develop tentative answers to such questions.

The context of the parable – sheep and shepherds in the Bible

An Old Testament overview

The Bible gives us a great wealth of material concerning sheep and other livestock and their keepers; many of its writings emerge from a culture of subsistence pastoralism, practised since before the days of Abraham and Sarah, up to the time of Jesus.

- Genesis locates animal husbandry right back at the beginning of the human story, presenting Abel, the second son of Adam and Eve, as a herdsman (Genesis 4:2), while his brother Cain was a 'tiller of the ground'.
- Abraham and his nephew Lot were so 'rich in livestock' (Genesis 13:2) they had to split up because the land could not support their huge herds.
- When Jacob and his sons came to settle in Egypt during the famine, they were granted land based on their need:

    Pharaoh said to [Joseph's] brothers, 'What is your occupation?' And they said to Pharaoh, 'Your servants are shepherds, as our ancestors were.'   *Genesis 47:3*

75

- Hundreds of years later, Moses left a long-standing role as a shepherd to go to Egypt, to the enslaved descendants of Joseph's brothers.
- The Bible also tells us about women who were shepherds. Moses first met his future wife Zipporah at a well where she and her sisters were tending their father's flock (Exodus 2:16). Jacob, too, met his future wife Rachel at a well, as he was talking with local men:

    While he was still speaking with them, Rachel came with her father's sheep; for she kept them. *Genesis 29:9*

- Even the 'beloved' of the Song of Songs has a flock; she is told to pasture them near the shepherds' tents (Song of Songs 1:8).

Shepherd as metaphor of leadership

With such a strong pastoral tradition, it is not surprising to find the shepherd frequently used as a metaphor for leaders of people, and also for God. Perhaps the most famous is in Psalm 23, which we considered earlier.

    The Lord is my shepherd, I shall not want.
    He makes me lie down in green pastures;
    he leads me beside still waters;
    he restores my soul.
    He leads me in right paths
    for his name's sake.   *Psalm 23:1-3*

For reflection

- What is your response to Psalm 23? (It is printed in full at the start of the introduction.)

Lost sheep

There are particular references to lost sheep in the Hebrew Scriptures. One example is the last verse of Psalm 119 which reads as a plea from a person who feels a direct, meaningful and personal relationship with God, which can still speak for us today:

I have gone astray like a lost sheep;
seek out your servant,
for I do not forget your commandments.

Psalm 119:176

Then in Jeremiah 50:6, 7, from a time in which many of the people of Israel and Judea were in exile in Babylon, we read:

My people have been lost sheep; their shepherds have led them astray, turning them away on the mountains; from mountain to hill they have gone, they have forgotten their fold. All who found them have devoured them, and their enemies have said, 'We are not guilty, because they have sinned against the Lord, the true pasture, the Lord, the hope of their ancestors.'

This time, the shepherds are not identified as God but as incompetent leaders of the people. The sheep are lost because of the leaders' failure. The metaphor that describes God here, is the 'true pasture' – a safe place, a source of abundant sustenance for the sheep, the environment in which they live.

This passage is a very helpful reminder that we cannot contain God with our titles and metaphors. One minute the Bible talks of God as a Shepherd, the next as a grassy field! Elsewhere in the Bible we read, among other things, that God is a strong rock (Psalm 19:14), a safe refuge (Psalm 57:1

and 34:22), a shield (Genesis 15:1) or a devouring fire (Deuteronomy 4:24). While this book mainly explores the idea of the Shepherd, God of course is infinitely more, unbound by our attempts at defining and labelling.

For reflection
• Of the images listed above – true pasture, strong rock, safe refuge – how do you feel about relating to God as an environment or a place?

Good shepherd bad shepherd, good sheep bad sheep
Jeremiah uses the imagery of sheep and shepherds several times, but the most developed use is in Ezekiel 34. God, through the prophet, starts by criticising the leaders of the people as false shepherds who feast on the sheep but neglect them. It is worth reading the whole chapter, but I have singled out some extracts:

First, we read about the lost sheep, sorely let down by the leadership:

> You eat the fat, you clothe yourselves with the wool, you slaughter the fatlings; but you do not feed the sheep. You have not strengthened the weak, you have not healed the sick, you have not bound up the injured, you have not brought back the strayed, you have not sought the lost, but with force and harshness you have ruled them. So they were scattered, because there was no shepherd; and scattered, they became food for all the wild animals.   *Ezekiel 34:3-5*

We might ask how this relates to our own times – as perhaps people did in Jesus' day.

The voice of God continues:

I will rescue my sheep from their mouths, so that they
may not be food for them.

For thus says the Lord God: I myself will search for
my sheep, and will seek them out. As shepherds seek
out their flocks when they are among their scattered
sheep, so I will seek out my sheep.   *Ezekiel 34:10-12*

Reading the whole, we see that the sheep here are the
scattered and exiled Hebrew people, dispossessed after the
invasion and conquest of their homeland. God is expressing
compassion for the people, who will be regathered and
restored.

In verse 15, God declares, in words that reflect Psalm 23, 'I
myself will be the shepherd of my sheep, and I will make
them lie down.'

For reflection

• What injustices do you see in the world and in your
own life which reflect Ezekiel's description of bad
shepherds?

Next, the theme shifts as the flock itself comes under
scrutiny. Within it, God sees a mixture of characters:

Therefore, thus says the Lord God to them: I myself
will judge between the fat sheep and the lean sheep.
Because you pushed with flank and shoulder, and
butted at all the weak animals with your horns until
you scattered them far and wide, I will save my flock,
and they shall no longer be ravaged; and I will judge
between sheep and sheep.   *Ezekiel 34:20-22*

It is bullying behaviour within the flock itself – abuse of
power, greed, selfishness and aggressiveness; in short,

violence against others – that God opposes. The community matters, and within it the needs of the vulnerable are to be protected.

Next comes a declaration that Christians through the ages have found meaningful in interpreting the role of Jesus. Perhaps Jesus himself felt this passage defined his identity and role:

> I will set up over them one shepherd, my servant David, and he shall feed them: he shall feed them and be their shepherd. And I, the Lord, will be their God, and my servant David shall be prince among them; I, the Lord, have spoken.   *Ezekiel 34:23, 24*

For reflection
• How do you respond to this passage?

What comes next is a vision of peace, freedom and prosperity for the people who have been returned to the land, now enhanced by a perfected environment in which the rains and the crops never fail and there is no more threat of invasion or attack. Such an existence seems incredible on earth as we know it, subject as we are to climatic fluctuations and hostility between peoples. In Ezekiel's vision, this is a changed, healed earth (not unlike that of Isaiah 11:1-11). Is it a vision of heaven on earth? Is it an insight into the 'kingdom of God'?

> I will send down the showers in their season; they shall be showers of blessing. The trees of the field shall yield their fruit, and the earth shall yield its increase. They shall be secure on their soil; and they shall know that I am the Lord, when I break the bars of their yoke, and save them from the hands of those who enslaved them.

They shall no more be plunder for the nations, nor shall the animals of the land devour them; they shall live in safety, and no one shall make them afraid.

Ezekiel 34:26-28

A summary of Ezekiel 34

This extended passage from Ezekiel gives us a great deal to think about concerning sheep and shepherds. It is a passage that was clearly known to and used by Jesus and his listeners and by the writers of the Gospels. We might draw out six points in particular:

1. Our understanding of God as shepherd is affirmed.
2. We see God's compassion for those who go astray for want of proper care and leadership.
3. We hear that God calls those in power to account: God's concern is with justice and the needs of the most vulnerable.
4. God also has a concern for the way in which members of the flock treat one another, particularly with regard to use and abuse of power and compassion for the vulnerable.
5. As Christians, we find meaning in identifying Jesus as the Good Shepherd sent by God, as we put ourselves under his protection and guidance.
6. We can find hope in the vision of restoration, healing and peace.

You might like to pause and look up some of the passages I have referred to for yourself, to see them in their proper context and to reflect further.

The Gospels

Jesus, being Jewish, was rooted in the Scriptures we have explored above. He, too, used images of sheep and shepherds in his teaching. There are many references to sheep and lambs in the New Testament. I have tried to focus particularly on lost sheep.

- In Mark 6:34/Matthew 9:36 we read that Jesus had compassion on the crowd because they were 'like sheep without a shepherd'.
- The writer of Matthew's Gospel twice records Jesus as declaring his mission to be 'to the lost sheep of the house of Israel' (10:6; 15:24). We might see a connection with the words of the prophets above in their concern for God's people who had been neglected or ill-treated by their leaders. Jesus has a concern for ordinary people who are struggling to feel close to God in their lives because of oppressive conditions imposed on them.
- As he faces death, Jesus is described as quoting from the prophet Zechariah (13:7), likening the desertion of the disciples to the behaviour of sheep:

    When they had sung the hymn, they went out to the Mount of Olives. And Jesus said to them, 'You will all become deserters; for it is written, "I will strike the shepherd, and the sheep will be scattered."'

    Mark 14:26, 27

Jesus understands his followers' weaknesses and fears; he anticipates them and forgives them. He understands our weaknesses and fears and forgives us, too.

Again, you might like to look up some of these passages in the Bible, to consider their context and think about what they say to you personally. A particularly lengthy section on the subject of sheep and shepherds is found in chapter 10 of John's Gospel. Here is an extract:

I am the good shepherd. The good shepherd lays down his life for the sheep. The hired hand, who is not the shepherd and does not own the sheep, sees the wolf coming and leaves the sheep and runs away – and the wolf snatches them and scatters them. The hired hand runs away because a hired hand does not care for the sheep. I am the good shepherd. I know my own and my own know me, just as the Father knows me and I know the Father. And I lay down my life for the sheep.

John 10:11-15

As with so much of John's Gospel, this passage leaves us with many questions concerning its meaning, and we might find ourselves identifying with some aspects of it more strongly than others. How do you read it? What is the wolf? Who is the hired hand? Who are the ones known by the shepherd? Who is the shepherd? Is this an allusion to the caring leader of God's people, described in Ezekiel 34:23, 24 above? Does it matter? Or is it enough simply to hear the devotion of the good shepherd to his flock?

For further reflection

- As well as being the Good Shepherd, Jesus is also called the Lamb of God. This seems to relate to the sacrificial lambs offered up in the Temple. A shepherd singles out lambs from the flock for this purpose, yet Jesus steps forward himself, the willing victim. What do you make of this?
- How do we choose our human shepherds?
- What qualities do we expect of them, and are our expectations always reasonable?

FOUR

Getting personal –
identifying with the lost sheep

Am I a lost sheep?

Like it or not, most of us feel like a lost sheep at some point
in our lives – if not at some point every day – straying away
from the love of God and perhaps the flock too. In this
chapter, we will think about our own experiences in relation
to the parable Jesus told.

The innocent victim

Some biblical passages referring to sheep are about innocent
victims who are mistreated by people who have power over
them. So a lost sheep could represent someone who feels
they have been

- led astray
- let down
- betrayed
- ignored
- exploited
- abused by those with power over them.

This can include feelings we carry with us from childhood.
Thinking about the biblical characters in the previous
chapter, we might see Hagar as belonging to this group.
Perhaps you have felt like this at times in your life. We might
see the same experience in the life of Jesus himself. A well-
known passage, often used by Christians since the earliest
times to make sense of Jesus' death, is that of the suffering
servant in Isaiah:

> He was oppressed, and he was afflicted,
> yet he did not open his mouth;
> like a lamb that is led to the slaughter,
> and like a sheep that before its shearers is silent,
> so he did not open his mouth.   *Isaiah 53:7*

The sinner

In contrast to this 'victim' identity, the writer of Luke's Gospel equates lostness with sinfulness, departure from God for personal and moral reasons, when we do something which we are ashamed of. So the lost sheep represents someone who feels

- guilty
- ashamed
- embarrassed
- confused
- judged
- condemned
- humiliated

and who is actively involved in an activity which they and/or others believe to be unacceptable in some way to God and/or to the community.

Which of the biblical characters in the previous chapter might identify with this group? Jacob? The young Moses?

It is important for us in this situation to know that the parable of the good shepherd is especially true for us in our sinfulness. God really does rejoice, the Gospel says, over the restoration of a 'sinner'. God seeks us out, lifts us up and brings us back to the fold.

The fearful and the failure

With regard to Jesus' prophetic words that his disciples will scatter like sheep when he is captured, we might also include the experiences of those who feel

- abandoned
- threatened
- frightened
- disillusioned
- confused

and those who feel they have

- let God down
- betrayed God or those close to them
- failed.

The disciples, especially Peter, fall into this group.

Sometimes these feelings draw us closer to God, because that is where we find our comfort, but sometimes they drive us away. Perhaps there have been times when you, too, have experienced some of these feelings.

The 'hidden' lostness of moral superiority

There is another way of being 'lost'. Several times, Jesus makes the point that it is those who believe themselves to be safe because of their own moral superiority who risk being furthest from God. They cut themselves off from help because they think they are doing fine on their own: they don't need God's grace and mercy because they have not (or believe they have not) done anything wrong. We read of such characters, caricatured as 'scribes and Pharisees', but 'they' are 'us' when we become so sure of our own righteousness compared with the sins of others that we cannot love.

When we have no love for others, as it says in 1 John 4:20, 21, then we have no genuine love of God either:

Those who say, 'I love God', and hate their brothers or sisters, are liars; for those who do not love a brother or sister whom they have seen, cannot love God whom they have not seen. The commandment we have from him is this: those who love God must love their brothers and sisters also.

How far are we from God if we have no love? Again, as Paul tells us in 1 Corinthians 13 – referred to earlier on – without love we are nothing. And what is love?

> Love is patient; love is kind; love is not envious or boastful or arrogant or rude. It does not insist on its own way; it is not irritable or resentful; it does not rejoice in wrongdoing, but rejoices in the truth. It bears all things, believes all things, hopes all things, endures all things.   *1 Corinthians 13:4-7*

That position of pride and self-confidence in our own worthiness may feel strong, but it is actually an insecure place to be. The Gospels frequently describe how 'tax-collectors' and 'prostitutes' – that is, those who fit the conventional idea of a 'sinner' – are turning and entering the kingdom of heaven ahead of the righteous because they hear the voice of the Shepherd, love it and draw close. The ones who are at risk are those who cannot hear the voice, yet these, too, are held in God's love. Jesus the Good Shepherd does not just go to obvious lost sheep – he also goes to the invisible lost, who don't even realise they are lost at all. Sometimes they don't respond, but sometimes they do.

A Gospel example of 'hidden' lostness:
One of the Pharisees asked Jesus to eat with him, and he went into the Pharisee's house and took his place at the table. And a woman in the city, who was a sinner, having learned that he was eating in the Pharisee's house, brought an alabaster jar of ointment. She stood behind him at his feet, weeping, and began to bathe his

feet with her tears and to dry them with her hair. Then she continued kissing his feet and anointing them with the ointment. Now when the Pharisee who had invited him saw it, he said to himself, 'If this man were a prophet, he would have known who and what kind of woman this is who is touching him – that she is a sinner.' Jesus spoke up and said to him, 'Simon, I have something to say to you.' 'Teacher,' he replied, 'speak.' 'A certain creditor had two debtors; one owed five hundred denarii, and the other fifty. When they could not pay, he cancelled the debts for both of them. Now which of them will love him more?' Simon answered, 'I suppose the one for whom he cancelled the greater debt.' And Jesus said to him, 'You have judged rightly.' Then turning towards the woman, he said to Simon, 'Do you see this woman? I entered your house; you gave me no water for my feet, but she has bathed my feet with her tears and dried them with her hair. You gave me no kiss, but from the time I came in she has not stopped kissing my feet. You did not anoint my head with oil, but she has anointed my feet with ointment. Therefore, I tell you, her sins, which were many, have been forgiven; hence she has shown great love. But the one to whom little is forgiven, loves little.' Then he said to her, 'Your sins are forgiven.' But those who were at the table with him began to say among themselves, 'Who is this who even forgives sins?' And he said to the woman, 'Your faith has saved you; go in peace.'   *Luke 7:36-50*

In the account above, Jesus dines with Simon, a respected member of the community who is described as a Pharisee. By that, we might understand him to be a person trying to live every detail of his life according to the principles of his faith in a way that keeps him ever mindful of God and by which he hopes to please God. Put this way, perhaps he is not so very different from many of us, as we try to live according to our own faith. In relation to the parable of the lost sheep, we might see Simon as one of the well-behaved flock who has never strayed; he may even see himself like that too.

Into the scene comes a controversial character – 'a woman in the city, who was a sinner'. We don't know the nature of her sin, but it seems that both Simon and Jesus do. This woman might seem like the obvious person to cast as a lost sheep – yet notice that she has sought Jesus out, not the other way around: she recognises the voice of the Shepherd and knows he is safe; it is the rest of the flock she has problems with, as we soon see.

Next, we witness two reactions: the way of condemnation, rejection and harsh judgement, intended to ostracise, versus the way of compassion, acceptance, gentleness, welcome and forgiveness, intended to restore dignity. The first way, as Jesus points out to Simon, comes from a lack of experience of God's grace. Jesus the Good Shepherd not only welcomes the woman to him but also shields her from this rather overbearing 'sheep', Simon, so that she can come back into the fold.

But who, all the way through the episode, is the furthest from God? Who is the most lacking in love? Who has Jesus come to dine with and talk to, who doesn't even know he needs help? Who has the Shepherd come to? Is it not Simon? We find something similar when Jesus invites himself to dinner with another influential figure – Zacchaeus the tax collector. This time, it is more clear that Zacchaeus is the one who needs help, and when Jesus comes to him, his change from lost to found is sudden and dramatic. (This story is found in Luke 19:1-10.)

Love is of crucial importance and goes hand in hand with forgiveness. During the meal at which the woman weeps at Jesus' feet, Jesus tells his host Simon, 'I tell you, her sins, which were many, have been forgiven; hence she has shown great love. But the one to whom little is forgiven, loves little' (Luke 7:47).

Having received great love, the woman can show great love. Her heart has been opened by God's merciful grace so that she now experiences a deep intimacy with God, and this is expressed by her bathing of Jesus' feet. Who is loveless? The loveless are the ones who cut themselves off from God.

The account of the dinner with Simon suggests that we are loveless when we point the finger, exclude, revile, pick fault, pass judgement, disdain, withhold respect or condemn others from our own position of presumed righteousness. This is a challenge that can be very difficult to hear – as some people in Jesus' day found. Perhaps what made it all the more uncomfortable was the way a woman (as in other Gospel situations) was presented as the person in right, faithful relationship with Jesus, while the male authority figure was in a state of disharmony.

I would suggest, then, that we could also be described as lost sheep when we display a lack of love for others, because we have distanced ourselves from God's way. We may be lost if we feel

- superior
- proud
- hostile
- sure of our own righteousness
- a lack of respect for another person
- judgemental
- intolerant
- that we see their faults more clearly than our own.

According to the Gospels, the difference between this list and the previous ones is that in this state we are less likely to welcome the Good Shepherd when he comes, and more likely to reject him, because from this position we hear not words of forgiveness and healing but a challenge that we do not like. If we cannot respond to the Good Shepherd's corrective with humility and loving gratitude, then we keep ourselves outside the love of God. We build up our barriers. We choose to stay lost.

Living in hope

All the feelings and experiences I have listed above are a familiar part of being a human being. As people of faith, we are not immune to the experience of that valley of shadows that is described in Psalm 23; in fact, it can become our greatest of teachers. It is not that a Christian never experiences low points, but faith gives confidence that God can and will enter, work with and transform those difficulties – we will experience the restoration of our souls. We are God's sheep and we will not be forgotten or abandoned; rather, we will be lifted up and brought back in joy. This is our hope.

What stops us receiving the love that God offers to us? Our own suspicion, our pride, our sense of unworthiness or pain . . . It is we who choose whether to accept or reject. But the outstretched hand of help is not offered only once and never again; God is continuously pouring out love and waits with infinite patience for each of us to turn and be loved, and so to love. Even in the most difficult of circumstances, God's presence can be experienced in moments of love.

But do not ignore this one fact, beloved, that with the Lord one day is like a thousand years, and a thousand years are like one day. The Lord is not slow about his promise, as some think of slowness, but is patient with you, not wanting any to perish, but all to come to repentance.   *2 Peter 3:8, 9*

For reflection
• What are your own thoughts and experiences of lostness? Which of the instances above did you identify with most strongly?

Divine and human qualities of a shepherd

Early Christian mosaics portray Christ as a shepherd relaxing in green pasture land, with the starry heavens stretching out beyond, exuding a deep tranquillity. We are left wondering whether they depict an earthly scene or a vision of paradise. Idyllic, far removed from the noise and concrete of our cities, perhaps they seem inaccessible at times, but they deserve a second glance. They are an iconic touching point where it becomes possible for us to experience God's love, proclaimed through a healed creation in the here and now.

In Jeremiah 50:6, 7, as we read above, the pasture is a metaphor for God. The shepherd and sheep in this pasture are at peace 'in' God. The Shepherd – another metaphor for God – reassures us that God is for us, not against us, and that God's creation, our home, is good and wholesome. Yes, it is broken and waiting to be 'set free from the bondage of decay' (Romans 8:18-25) and yes, a little like its maker, it is wilder and greater than humanity and therefore potentially frightening as well as beautiful. But creation is good, because God is its creator, and God declares it to be good.

The good shepherd displays qualities which tell us about God, but also about humanity. At our best, we develop qualities which reflect divine goodness. We are capable of great compassion, courage, wisdom, gentleness and selflessness. Recognising these qualities in one another, even in embryo form, helps us to know something of God, who is infinitely more compassionate, wise and self-giving. God grows within us in the depth of our hearts.

The shepherd of those early Christian scenes is someone who seeks out the scattered and lost, who has a concern for the vulnerable, for those who have been let down, exploited or misled by others, and those who feel cut off from the community of God. He (or she – remember we can have female shepherds) brings justice and mercy, challenging those who stray away through self-interest. The shepherd brings forgiveness and healing, protecting our souls from harm, knowing what is best for each of us. He leads and directs with wisdom. The shepherd is the flock's carer, helping each ewe at birth and knowing each lamb that is born, watching it grow.

When we look to our own human leaders, and when we take on leadership roles ourselves, qualities such as those listed above are crucial. The passages from Ezekiel and Jeremiah warn us of the dangers of corrupt leadership, of bad shepherds who exploit and neglect, caring only for their own gain. They also warn us of bullying behaviours between sheep, where some grow fat at the expense of others, and they challenge our capacity for violence.

For reflection

- When have you found yourself as protector and guardian of something or someone precious?

Human leadership

Our attitude to leaders, leadership and people in authority generally can sometimes be part of our struggle. Many of us grow up with 'issues' about father figures and mother figures which we transfer on to people in positions of responsibility, and also on to God. Here lie the roots of anxieties about not being good enough, about the threat of punishment, of confusion about love, power dynamics and so much more.

According to the Gospels, Jesus taught and demonstrated a radical attitude to leadership, saying:

> You know that among the Gentiles those whom they recognise as their rulers lord it over them, and their great ones are tyrants over them. But it is not so among you; but whoever wishes to become great among you must be your servant, and whoever wishes to be first among you must be slave of all. *Mark 10:42-44*

The history of the Church shows how difficult followers of Jesus have often found this – but not always. There have also been remarkable people noted for their sense of humility and ability to lead others through example and service rather than 'lording it'. One such was St Francis of Assisi who, in establishing a rule for his friars, made a point of describing ministers in positions of responsibility over others as 'also servants'. He also pointed out (being a devout Roman Catholic) that although priests in particular were to be given great respect, this was because of their office of administering the body and blood of Christ and not because of their human nature. They were likely to be as flawed as the next person.

We might perhaps see George Fox, the founder of the Quakers, as another. He drew attention to the statement of equality in Matthew 23:8-10, which in his translation talked about 'masters' and 'brethren', emphasising each person's responsibility directly to God:

You have one teacher, and you are all students. And call no one your father on earth, for you have one Father – the one in heaven. Nor are you to be called instructors, for you have one instructor, the Messiah.

There has always been a quiet voice in our tradition which reminds us of Jesus' words neither to elevate one another nor to assume power for ourselves, but rather to become great through self-giving. We – leaders and followers alike – forget or ignore such advice to our disadvantage. As a leader, when we fail, it is tempting to cover our tracks in desperation rather than risk downfall from our pedestal. When our leaders fail, it is tempting to show little mercy – as though we wanted them to be better than us, less flawed, more divine. Perhaps deep down we wanted them to be our gods, visible and tangible, but that is asking too much of anybody.

It is not easy to be or to follow a human shepherd. We are always aspiring towards the divine qualities of leadership without having fully mastered them – because we are only human. When we look to other human beings with the expectation that they will do better than us in terms of these qualities, we risk disillusionment. Staying true to that ancient psalm, The *Lord* is my Shepherd, may give us more peace in the end.

FIVE

Relating to God – six reflections

As people of faith, how we relate to God affects how we engage with life itself. When we are able to trust and say with the psalmist, 'The Lord is my shepherd, I shall not want . . .' then our walk through green pastures and gloomy valleys feels very different from the times when we feel lost and cut off from the Shepherd. It is gaining or keeping that sense of trust that often seems to be the issue.

You may want to answer, 'Speak for yourself; I have never lost my trust.' A friend said something similar to me a little while ago, but more kindly, after I had described how I had gone through some difficult years. Yes, it is true that some people's faith is unshakeable all their lives. That's wonderful! But this is a book for people for whom it has not been so easy. Rather than feeling like a failure in the face of other people's great faith, we can reassure ourselves (without in turn starting to feel superior!) with the words we read earlier, in Mark 2:17:

> When Jesus heard this, he said to them, 'Those who are well have no need of a physician, but those who are sick; I have come to call not the righteous but sinners.'

Jesus has a special place in his heart for people who know they are weak, sinful, poor, uncertain and lost – that, I think, is the whole point of the parable of the lost sheep.

In the following pages, I explore some of the issues that can make us put up barriers to God, rather than taking them down.

Using the reflections

Each of the themes in this chapter uses the same progression from lost to found, as outlined below.

- Overview
- Prayer of a lost sheep
- Encountering the Shepherd
- Prayer of a found sheep

1. Overview

The overview summarises the theme of the reflection. Looking at the bigger picture gives us hope that there is always a way back to love.

2. Prayer of a lost sheep

The first prayer of each themed reflection is a personal prayer. These prayers are a little like some of the psalms, using a direct way of talking to God while wrestling with difficult feelings and situations.

Because these prayers have a personal nature, you might feel you can express your situation better in your own words or in some other creative way. If this is the case, please do so!

3. Encountering the Shepherd

In this section I share Scriptures which speak to me of God's desire to restore relationship. This makes them a rather personal choice, and it might be that different Scriptures come to mind for you. If this is the case, by all means reflect on and pray with those instead, and perhaps make a note of them in the margin or in a journal.

4. Prayer of a found sheep

Change comes in welcoming the Good Shepherd. The closing prayer acknowledges God's reassuring and healing presence and its effect on our lives. There is a contrast between the first prayer of the section – the prayer of a lost sheep – and this last one, demonstrating a shift from lost to found.

The prayers of a sheep who has been found, listened to, comforted and restored are prayers of gratitude and love. Prayer, I think, is always the primary course of action, the inspiration and the impetus for renewal. It provides answers and solutions, but in God's unfathomable way, not in our limited, cerebral ways. Prayer is the opening up to God that allows love to flow. It is the stepping aside that welcomes God into our lives. You may want to write your own prayers, or paint, or play them out in music, or in another way that enables you to express your heart and soul. Please do!

Health warning

Although these reflections are of a personal nature, you may belong to a group or a partnership in which it feels appropriate to support each other in working through them, rather than alone. I would suggest *not* using them 'cold' in a new group until sufficient trust, mutual respect and warmth have been built up for all the members to know that they are safe to talk about their feelings and experiences openly and without any sense of judgement. This can be a lot to ask of a group. I would also strongly advise having spiritually and emotionally mature members present in the group, who will be able to give appropriate attention to any issues that come up.

If deep and troubled feelings do surface, whether you are working alone or with another, it is always advisable to consult a professional or other trusted person who can offer appropriate support.

Please refer to the notes at the back of the book for suggestions on taking matters further.

Suggested format for a workshop or group session

Gather together.

About 10 minutes:
- Light a candle and invite someone to say an opening prayer.
- Briefly introduce the theme and explain how the session is going to unfold.
- Someone reads the overview.
- Someone else reads the prayer of the lost sheep.
- Pause for a few minutes in silence.

About 20 minutes:
- Ensure that everybody has a copy of the 'Encountering the Shepherd' section. The leader or another confident voice reads it out loud, slowly. Where there are biblical quotations, look them up in Bibles and take time to savour each quotation, reading it several times, suggesting that people listen to it with their eyes closed if they want to.
- Invite members of the group to read from different translations to obtain different perspectives. I have quoted from the NRSV, but often I also read the Jewish Study Bible for insights into the Old Testament, and other versions such as *The Inclusive Bible: The First Egalitarian Translation*.
- Take time to pause for reflection, and where there are questions, allow time for people to think and talk with a neighbour or discuss together as a group.
- Draw this section to a close by singing a simple song such as a Taizé chant or listening to appropriate music.

Five minutes or 50!:
- Read the final prayer of the found sheep. In some cases there are two prayers, so the group could divide, just choose one or read both.

- The group can end here, or you could go on to respond personally and creatively to the theme. Depending on inclinations within the group and the skills of the leaders, this could become a music, painting or dance workshop, a time outdoors in a garden or out in the community, or a creative writing session, or could use any other method that helps people to express themselves and explore their feelings.
- Close with the grace.

Themed reflections about relating to God
1. Afraid of God's anger

Overview

As a child, did you ever hide away for fear of punishment? Sometimes we can experience a childlike dread of God, brought on by the notion that we have done something 'wrong', for which we will be in trouble. Hiding in fear is one of the very first human behaviours described in the Book of Genesis: Adam and Eve hide in the foliage in an attempt to avoid God after they have eaten the forbidden fruit (Genesis 3:8).

Jesus told us that we can think of God as a parent. Does a loving father or mother want their child to live in dread of them? Images of children or creatures cowering in fear are sickening and awake our natural compassion. Do we really believe a God of love would wish for us to cower like that? Is this the way a wise and self-controlled parent treats their child, or a shepherd their sheep? No, wise carers moderate their behaviour and know what the appropriate response is for each situation, and always work for the good of the one in their care. We cannot domesticate God and expect only sweetness and light; there is serious work to do on

ourselves. But we can rely on God's goodness and, above
all, God's love, the drive towards reconciliation, healing
and renewal.

We cannot deny that the Bible describes God's wrath, but
it also describes God's tender mercy, and it is this mercy that
we are promised, through our faith.

Prayer of a lost sheep

I want to put myself in a place
where you can't find me.
I've got this image in my mind
of an angry teacher or a parent raging
because they've just heard something they don't like.
Now they know who it was
and they will teach them a lesson,
vent their anger, all that pent-up power,
so they're stomping around
like a giant in a fairy tale,
and all because of me.
So I'm hiding where I hope you can't find me,
because I am already sorry –
I don't need you to tell me –
and I am afraid of your power.

Encountering the Shepherd

In the Bible, frightening, chaotic power is often represented
by images of a stormy sea or flood waters. There is an
ancient tradition from the Bible lands that God wrestles with
these waters of chaos in order to restore stability and peace.
This is what Psalm 93 is celebrating:

> More majestic than the thunders of mighty waters,
> more majestic than the waves of the sea,
> majestic on high is the Lord!   *Psalm 93:4*

Psalm 69 is the prayer of someone in great distress, who says these fearful waters of chaos have come up to their neck and are sweeping away their foothold. Verse 5 gives us words for our own prayer:

O God, you know my folly;
the wrongs I have done are not hidden from you.

Yet the psalmist distinguishes between the dangerous waters and God's activity, feeling able to call for mercy despite the 'folly'. The waters are not God's punishment but represent the violence and turbulence of the world in which this person is caught up. Aware of their own imperfection, they still know they can call out for help.

But as for me, my prayer is to you, O Lord.
At an acceptable time, O God,
in the abundance of your steadfast love, answer me.
With your faithful help rescue me
from sinking in the mire.   *Psalm 69:13, 14*

Acknowledging our own imperfection, what prayer can we utter that overcomes our fear with hope?

Perhaps Peter reflected on this psalm as he tried to make sense of his own experiences. He is a character fully aware of his own shortcomings: 'Go away from me, Lord, for I am a sinful man!' he exclaims, one day at the beginning of Jesus' ministry, when faced with the miraculous catch of fish (Luke 5:8).

Then, 'Lord, save me!' he cries, when strong winds make him lose confidence and sink as he tries to walk out to Jesus on the water of the lake (Matthew 14:30).

When we are especially aware of our failings, we can be reassured that the destructive, frightening disturbance around us is not of God; the power of God is good, supportive and loving. This is good news, but it can elude us if we interpret safety only in physical terms. What Jesus says about safety and risk, willingness to die and the gift of eternal life is not a promise of a charmed existence; we are still mortal. The path of faith is a call to carry a cross – a risky business if ever there was one. Followers are warned that life will be hard. Jesus himself was not spared death. 'Safety' is a promise that, dying and living, our souls are held by God who loves us.

Prayer of a found sheep

Shepherding God, help me to trust that I am safe in your presence so that I can come out of this hiding place and stretch, and feel fully alive again. Thank you that your love for me is such that you will never hurt me but only help me. Reassure me that your power is supreme over everything else that troubles me and that your understanding of me is perfect, so that I need never fear, but only grow in respect, in awe and in gratitude for your compassion.

Amen.

2. Feeling angry with God

Overview

Choosing to see God as the one to blame for all our troubles, the troubles of those we love and the troubles of the world can lead to a real breakdown of relationship if it means we stop talking to God.

When Jesus told us we could call God 'Father', perhaps he was giving us permission to go through this process of raging at God. Ideally, children are safe in the knowledge that the most loving and wise of parents would never really take offence, but wait patiently for their son or daughter to see things differently.

God knows that there are plenty of reasons to be angry, from our position, as we see so much that seems wrong, even incomprehensible. Being angry, after all, can be a sign that we have a heart and are taking notice of the world around us.

But then, an angry heart is not just angry about worthy causes; an angry heart is provoked by the ordinary experiences of everyday life. We all know people who are passionately committed to doing good in the world but are so bitter and opinionated that nobody wants to join their cause. Unless the fuel for passionate action is compassionate love, it sparks and smokes threateningly; who knows when it will run out of control and against whom it will be directed next? When we talk about being angry with God, it is worth looking at everything else we are angry with, too – including ourselves – and it is worth sharing it all with God.

Prayer of a lost sheep

I'm so angry with you.
I just want to storm off
and have nothing more to do with you.
I feel that you really messed my life up.
I blame you for the things that have happened –
not just to me but to those I care about –
and I don't see how you can expect me
to love you or trust you any more.
Who else is there to blame?
You are the Creator, after all,
so why did you create things to be so difficult?
I thought you are God Most High, all powerful.
You can do anything, can't you?
So why have you done this?
Or rather, why have you *not* come to help?

If it's because you can't,
because your hands are tied,
I really don't see what use you are at all.

Encountering the Shepherd

There are a few characters in the Bible who lose their temper with God. Job is one. He is famous for having suffered greatly and undeservedly. A huge part of this suffering, especially the death of his children and loss of his servants and livestock, is shared by his wife. It seems she has chosen her response and says to Job, 'Do you still persist in your integrity? Curse God, and die' (Job 2:9).

At first, Job rather piously refuses to do such a thing. But later, provoked by his companions who suggest he is being punished, he does get angry:

> I cry to you and you do not answer me;
> I stand, and you merely look at me.
> You have turned cruel to me;
> with the might of your hand you persecute me.
> You lift me up on the wind, you make me ride on it,
> and you toss me about in the roar of the storm.

Job 30:20-22

Job's righteousness is the tipping point: he does not believe he deserves to suffer and decides he is being victimised. A chapter later, he challenges God to account for this injustice: 'Here is my signature! Let the Almighty answer me!' (Job 31:35). The last chapters of the book contain God's humbling answer.

Another who expresses anger is Jonah, whom we considered earlier. He is angry almost all the way through the book! He is angry that God sends him on a mission, then that God spares the people he has preached to because they to choose to repent:

But this was very displeasing to Jonah, and he became angry. He prayed to the Lord and said, 'O Lord! Is not this what I said while I was still in my own country? That is why I fled to Tarshish at the beginning; for I knew that you are a gracious God and merciful, slow to anger, and abounding in steadfast love, and ready to relent from punishing. And now, O Lord, please take my life from me, for it is better for me to die than to live.' And the Lord said, 'Is it right for you to be angry?'   *Jonah 4:1-4*

Then, storming off, Jonah shelters under a bush which God provides for him. When the bush is removed, he is angry again:

But God said to Jonah, 'Is it right for you to be angry about the bush?' And he said, 'Yes, angry enough to die.'   *Jonah 4:9*

What is interesting is that neither Job nor Jonah stop talking to God. They vent their feelings, but they also listen and hear God's response. They are still in dialogue, in relationship with God.

A third character who gets annoyed with God is Moses. When he and Aaron first go to Pharaoh to tell him to set the Hebrews free, Pharaoh increases the people's labour, and they complain to Moses for interfering:

Then Moses turned again to the Lord and said, 'O Lord, why have you mistreated this people? Why did you ever send me? Since I first came to Pharaoh to speak in your name, he has mistreated this people, and you have done nothing at all to deliver your people.'   *Exodus 5:22, 23*

God is patient with Moses, repeats the promise of deliverance and sends Moses back to Pharaoh to try again – which he does.

Job, Jonah and Moses all express anger with God, for reasons which seem quite reasonable. What happens? God contains the anger, giving each an appropriate response, and always showing the glimmer of a bigger reality which is beyond our comprehension. Job is not to know what will happen when his sickness ends. Jonah is not to know how much God cares for the inhabitants (including the animals) of the city. Moses is not to know that soon the ten plagues will be unleashed and an epic journey of 40 years will begin. They do not know what comes next, and neither do we, in our lives.

These characters show us that it is acceptable to tell God exactly how we feel. That is the first step. Try it. Try it every day. In time, you might find that God is listening. What happens next is between you and God.

How do you feel about being completely honest with God?

Prayer of a found sheep

Eternal One, I bring my anger to you, and I bring the pain that is causing my anger, and I ask you to hold all of this in your forgiving arms and give my heart rest. I know you love the compassion and the sense of justice that you see growing in me. I know you love me for the struggle I am undertaking to make sense of my life. But help me simply to trust that you are good and work in the hearts of your faithful, to bring about good, even in the midst of confusion and suffering. Kindle in my heart a flame of your love, O God, so that I may shine with hope and give hope through you to others.

Amen.

3. Feeling excluded

Overview

An increasing number of people feel unable to relate to God in Christian translations of Scripture and in worship because there is still such a strong emphasis on masculine language. It often seems that Christians believe in a wholly male God, which can make women in particular (although there are also men who prefer inclusive language) feel excluded, marginalised and even incapable of intimacy with God. I believe that this might be one reason why many today seek alternative spiritualities that offer emphasis on the feminine.

Yet Scripture and Christian thought through the ages make clear that God transcends and encompasses male and female; there is potential, historical precedent and scriptural justification for acknowledging the divine feminine (without excluding the masculine), and a great deal of work has been done in this field over the last few decades by leading theologians. For some reason, their work is taking a very long time to trickle into the thinking and worship of church communities. Why is this?

How can we delve into our own rich faith tradition for elements that might help all people feel close to God *within* rather than outside of the Church?

Prayer of a lost sheep

I thought you commanded us not to make images of you,
O God.
Father, Lord, King, Master, Son even:
these names create an image in my mind –
a mighty man, alpha male,
that I am supposed to bow down to.
But I thought male and female together are in your image,
not just male.

And I'm sure I read somewhere how you cried out like a
woman in labour,
how you nursed your children, loved them tenderly,
fed them with breast-milk until they were mature.
I thought I heard of Christ's death as the agony of labour,
of birthing us to new life.
I thought this was part of the great story,
but all I hear is 'He', 'Him', 'His'.
Is there a cover-up going on?
I'm sorry, God, but this is the twenty-first century
and it's time for equal opportunities.
I want to love you, to get to know you more deeply,
but I just feel much more comfortable
talking to a female about intimate things.
As it is, I just don't feel I can get close to you if you are
only 'He'.

Encountering the Shepherd

In Matthew 23:37 and Luke 13:34, Jesus talks about wanting
to gather the people of the city up in his care:

> Jerusalem, Jerusalem, the city that kills the prophets
> and stones those who are sent to it! How often have I
> desired to gather your children together as a hen gathers
> her brood under her wings, and you were not willing!'

Luke 13:34

Many hear a yearning and a tenderness in Jesus' voice, a
disappointment that his invitation to love is not welcomed.
Jesus the Good Shepherd is also the Mother Hen. Christian
thinkers of the past, such as Anselm and Julian of Norwich,
explored the idea of Jesus as our mother, likening his death
on the cross to labour pains and the sacrament of bread and
wine to milk.

In John 16:21, 22, Jesus talks about a woman's pain when 'her hour has come'. He says,

> When a woman is in labour, she has pain, because her hour has come. But when her child is born, she no longer remembers the anguish because of the joy of having brought a human being into the world. So you have pain now; but I will see you again, and your hearts will rejoice, and no one will take your joy from you.

A few verses later, in John 17:1, Jesus looks up to heaven and, addressing God, says, 'the hour has come.' But *what* hour? Is he still alluding to the woman above, whose labour pains he has described? Is birthing not a way that the gospel invites us to think about the cross?

How do you feel about this idea?

There are many metaphors for God in the Hebrew Scriptures. A number of these are feminine, such as Isaiah 66:13, where the voice of God says:

> As a mother comforts her child,
> so I will comfort you;
> you shall be comforted in Jerusalem.

God comforts in a feminine way.

In Psalm 131:1, 2, the psalmist describes sitting with God in prayer as being like a child sitting quietly on his or her mother's knee.

> I do not occupy myself with things
> too great and too marvellous for me.
> But I have calmed and quieted my soul,
> like a weaned child with its mother;
> my soul is like the weaned child that is with me.

Sitting with God in prayer, we can experience a loving feminine presence.

So what of the Holy Spirit? This, too, we find referred to as 'he' in many English translations of the Bible, but in Hebrew, the word commonly used for the Holy Spirit is *ruach* or *ruah*, meaning breath, wind or spirit of God, and it is a feminine word: *she* not *he* (although in languages where words have a gender this does not necessarily relate to sexuality). *Ruah* was translated into Greek as *pneumos*, which is neuter – genderless. But in Latin, which became the dominant language for a great deal of Western Christian history, the word is *spiritus* – which is masculine. Jesus, speaking Hebrew, was more likely to understand the Spirit as the feminine *ruah*. That means, I think, that we have some freedom ourselves to relate to the Holy Spirit in a feminine way if that helps us.

We find *ruah*, the breath or the wind of God, at the very beginning of the Bible:

> In the beginning when God created the heavens and the earth, the earth was a formless void and darkness covered the face of the deep, while a wind [ruah] from God swept over the face of the waters. *Genesis 1:1, 2*

How do you imagine that primordial scene, and what, to you, is the wind from God?

Prayers of a found sheep

Holy One, let me hear your voice in a way that makes me feel safe and included. Let me see you coming towards me like Rachel with her sheep, bold and strong, caring, generous and competent, with a kindly voice, firm yet gentle. Let me discover you anew, your all-encompassing, transcendent glory, your human tenderness and self-giving, your sacred, enlivening breath. Let me creep back into your care, rediscover your embrace, know for sure that your love includes me and that you want to draw me to you like a mother hen nestling her chicks.

Amen.

My Shepherd, thank you for drawing me into the fold of your love, for reaching out to me in a way that I can hear, for healing me from the feeling of exclusion, from the pain of feeling marginalised as though I am only second best. Thank you for raising me up in your eyes to be equal within your flock, equally beloved, equally valued. Open my heart to discover the depth of your perfect love for me, your nourishment and willingness to labour and die that I may live. Draw me to you and never let me go; reassure me that I need never stray in search of love, for you are all to me, and in you I find the words of eternal life.

Amen.

4. Did God leave me?

Overview

If we convince ourselves that we only 'have' God when we are feeling joyful and life is going well, then it is easy to walk away when that feeling fades. God is not just about the feel-good factor, and there is nothing superficial about the path Jesus showed us; it takes courage and commitment.

Sometimes we experience spiritual 'highs' when a euphoria lifts us up and transforms our lives. These moments are precious and can give us great strength during more difficult periods. We can experience confusion, however, if we believe that God *is* the feeling of joy or of warmth that has given us such a lift. God is bigger than our moods, feelings and emotions. God is present with us even when we feel low, and does not disappear or wear off like the effects of a drug. To endure, our faith needs to be built on more than a feeling. It is in those low points, those gloomy valleys, that our faith in the Shepherd can make all the difference.

Prayer of a lost sheep

I thought you were a feeling of joy,
a euphoria holding me up,
helping me shine out as a light in the world.
I thought you were like a power source,
keeping me burning strong.
But that warmth in me has petered out,
a bonfire put out by the rain,
and now the feeling's gone.
I'm empty, even exhausted,
and I don't know what to think any more.
Have you abandoned me?
Have you withdrawn your Spirit?
Is there something I don't understand?

Encountering the Shepherd

In the natural world, we see how a great surge of energy is often followed by a lull. Crashing waves will eventually recede. A storm will abate, the glaring sun will inevitably set, both hunter and hunted must stop running in the end, to rest. Much as we might love the thrill of spiritual highs, we have to accept that they will be balanced by what can seem like low points. These, too, are part of the spiritual process. We might not like them so much, but they can be times of great depth and renewal if we see them for what they are. We may even start to tire of the exhausting process of vacillating between feelings of elation and dull emptiness and start to seek a more balanced, calmer way of living in Christ.

In the parable of the sower, Jesus describes some different ways in which people respond to the word of God. According to Matthew 13:20, 21, he says:

As for what was sown on rocky ground, this is the one who hears the word and immediately receives it with joy; yet such a person has no root, but endures only for a while, and when trouble or persecution arises on account of the word, that person immediately falls away.

'Such a person has no root.' Of course, the roots of a plant are all-important to draw up water and nutrients and to act as anchors. In our faith, we are like plants growing towards God and in God, and we need nourishment, 'living water' and solid support if we are to thrive. Pause for a while and reflect on your own sources of spiritual nourishment. What feeds you and sustains you, keeps you strong, helps you grow?

What holds you firm in your faith so that even in difficult times, you know you will get through?

Perhaps your answers include some of the following:

- the companionship and inspiring example of others
- the memory of a powerful personal experience
- the tradition and sense of history
- the liturgy, prayer and worship
- receiving the Eucharist
- being part of a movement that is a force for good in the world
- the guidance of a helpful preacher, minister, songwriter or author
- following a rule of life or personal commitment to a group
- the Bible

All these things, and more, we might associate with the soil that helps us to endure. Not all soil has the same

115

composition; not everybody's faith has the same balance of elements, and that is part of the joy of diversity.

What are your own experiences of the diversity within our faith?

Looking at the list above, which elements mean more to you? Which seem really foreign to your own experience?

Grain and fruit are cultivated for us to eat. There, too, is a pointer to our spiritual development; it is not just to make us feel good. We are to bear fruit that is good for others. So many of the teachings of Jesus talk about this organic growth of grain and fruit trees, and of course the vine:

> My Father is glorified by this, that you bear much fruit
> and become my disciples. As the Father has loved me,
> so I have loved you; abide in my love.   *John 15:8*

Our fruit is to the glory of God, but it is also by God's work. Jesus the vine tells us how God continuously refines even him so that he bears only the very best grapes for the very best wine. This refinement process is part of the spiritual journey, or growing in God's love. Being pruned is not much fun; it is the serious work of maturing us to be truly useful.

> I am the true vine, and my Father is the vine-grower.
> He removes every branch in me that bears no fruit.
> Every branch that bears fruit he prunes to make it bear
> more fruit.   *John 15:1, 2*

Choosing to follow Jesus is a commitment. He challenges us to take up our cross. It is often a path that includes suffering. These are hard truths that have caused many would-be followers to turn away, and we can choose to turn away too if it seems too much like hard work. But words of hope keep us going.

> You prepare a table before me
> in the presence of my enemies . . .
> and I shall dwell in the house of the Lord
> my whole life long.   *Psalm 23:5, 6*

A future is promised to us, a place at the table, and our present moment is attended to: our home even now is the house of the Lord. We belong to God and are being led, nurtured, trained, guided and shepherded towards full inclusion in God's kingdom. But we have not finished the process yet – that great joy is a future hope. For now, we may be blessed with moments of elation, but they are just an appetiser for what is to come.

Prayer of a found sheep

Oh my Shepherd, thank you for the times when you lift me up and fill me with joy. Let the memory of those moments live on in my soul like a flame, to gladden me and give me hope. Thank you also for the times of withdrawal, of calm, of quietness and emptiness, when I have to look more deeply within myself for the faith you have given me. Thank you that you are with me no matter how I feel, just as the shepherd is always watching over the flock. Help me to understand how to walk with you and to sense your presence with me even when everything seems flat, when the excitement has died down, when ordinariness takes hold, when it's just a matter of plodding on, patiently following, until the next green pasture comes into view. Give me a sense of peace, O God, as I learn to follow you over bright, high hills and low, gloomy valleys.

Amen.

5. I don't deserve God's love

Overview

It can seem to us that we are particularly bad, and rather than wait for the divine displeasure that we imagine is coming our way, we cut ourselves off first. The emphasis is not so much on the fear of punishment but on the sense of unworthiness. Our self-imposed punishment is severance from God as we tell ourselves that God does not want us any more because we have failed. In this state, when the promise of forgiveness is uttered, we find it very difficult to believe that it applies to us.

This outlook can be mistaken for an expression of great humility, but the sheer joylessness of it shows us that it is not of God. It is actually an expression of inverted self-importance as we dare to suggest that we of all people have pushed God's loving mercy further than it is able to go. Our sin has outfoxed God's grace. Our failure is greater than God's power and goodness. Can this really be possible?

Our reason for making the decision to stay outside of relationship with God is sometimes that we cannot bring ourselves to accept the love that is offered to us. God has compassion on us when we enter such a difficult place and knows our inner struggle. Believing ourselves unlovable is not so much a 'bad' notion as a very sad one.

Prayer of a lost sheep

I cannot believe you want anything to do with me now,
O God.
I've proved I'm not capable of being good and holy;
I've messed up my life so badly,
and the lives of other people too.
I don't see how you can still want me.
I'll just give your people a bad name.

There's no point in me trying to be anything other than
what I am –
a no-good sinner –
so I'm keeping out of the way.
I don't fit in anyway;
everyone else seems to find it a whole lot easier than I do
to be good and well-behaved.
I just can't keep it up,
and the sense of failing over and over again
is breaking me down.

Encountering the Shepherd

Jesus welcomes little children.

> People were bringing little children to him in order that
> he might touch them; and the disciples spoke sternly to
> them. But when Jesus saw this, he was indignant and
> said to them, 'Let the little children come to me; do not
> stop them; for it is to such as these that the kingdom of
> God belongs. Truly I tell you, whoever does not receive
> the kingdom of God as a little child will never enter it.'
> And he took them up in his arms, laid his hands on
> them, and blessed them. *Mark 10:13-16*

Inside, each of us carries the child we used to be. Some are
quite healthy and cause very little bother, allowing us to get
on with being mature adults in peace. Others show themselves in temper outbursts, whining, sulking and other, even
worse, 'childish' behaviours that we struggle to shake off.

You can bring your inner child to Jesus to receive
his blessing.

Are there voices that try to stop you?

Jesus gives a clear message that every child matters, and
he gives them all the love they need, the love their parents
want for them.

Each of us begins as a child, just like those in this crowd who were brought to receive Jesus' blessing. What happens over the years that makes us think we are no longer welcomed by Jesus? Which sinful, broken, remorseful, hurting person does Jesus ever turn away?

In Luke 15:11-32, Jesus tells a parable about a young man who decides he has crossed the line and is no longer worthy of his father's love. The son has the cheek to ask for his share of the inheritance while his father is still alive and goes off to spend it. When the money dries up, he finds himself friendless in a foreign land and is forced to take a humiliating job which does not earn him enough to eat. In the end, he decides that he would be better off working for his father. He sets off home, planning to say:

> Father, I have sinned against heaven and before you; I am no longer worthy to be called your son; treat me like one of your hired hands.   *Luke 15:18, 19*

The father will hear none of it and welcomes the boy back joyously. What is Jesus telling us about relationship with God in this parable?

What does it say to you personally?

The father closes the episode by exclaiming words of joy which echo those of the shepherd in the parable of the lost sheep, earlier in the same chapter.

> But we had to celebrate and rejoice, because this brother of yours was dead and has come to life; he was lost and has been found.   *Luke 15:32*

He was lost and has been found. This is a reason for celebration – that God loves us and desires our return; nobody is excluded from God's love because of what they have done, unless they choose to exclude themselves. God is not the one we should be hiding from, but is rather the safe refuge to which we can run.

Prayer of a found sheep

Oh my Shepherd, thank you that you love me. What more can I say? You accept me, you understand me, you comfort me and welcome me. When I run to you, you receive me. When I hide in you, you shelter me. Even in my loneliest times you are with me. When I stray furthest, you still know where to seek me out. Nothing I can do separates me from your love.

Amen.

6. I haven't got time

Overview

Some people thrive on being busy and, if they have a faith, seem to find a way for their activity to be a living prayer, an expression of love in action. The rest of us sometimes wonder how they do it, because keeping up with the demands of life as well as keeping in touch with God can be very difficult – in fact, as difficult as maintaining significant human relationships amidst the pressures of modern life. The truth is that not all relationships do survive; many of us live with the pain of brokenness. But what of God? What does it really say about us and our lives when we squeeze out the One we are told to love with all our heart and mind and being?

Prayer of a lost sheep

I am busy, O God,
trying to make ends meet, trying to stay on top of everything,
trying to get through my tick-list of things to do,

trying to keep up with the deadlines,
to please the boss,
to fulfil my obligations,
to earn a living,
to meet schedules,
to have a little time out every now and then to just relax.
This is the modern world;
it's fast and we have to keep up
to get ahead.
That's why I haven't got time for you.
Show me where in my diary
I'm supposed to fit in prayer time,
let alone a retreat.
If you want to talk to me,
best to send me a text.
Do you text, O God?

Encountering the Shepherd

Whenever the following reading comes up in church, some people are likely to go home feeling irritated:

> Now as they went on their way, he entered a certain village, where a woman named Martha welcomed him into her home. She had a sister named Mary, who sat at the Lord's feet and listened to what he was saying. But Martha was distracted by her many tasks; so she came to him and asked, 'Lord, do you not care that my sister has left me to do all the work by myself? Tell her then to help me.' But the Lord answered her, 'Martha, Martha, you are worried and distracted by many things; there is need of only one thing. Mary has chosen the better part, which will not be taken away from her.'
>
> *Luke 10:38-42*

The response for many of us – women and men – is to feel a great deal of sympathy for Martha. There is Jesus (whom so many laud as the 'first feminist'), generously allowing a woman to sit *at his feet* – not on a level – to *listen*, not debate – while her sister is frantically rushing around trying to cater for a whole entourage of hungry fishermen and the like, who are presumably also sitting around waiting to be fed. To be fair, this is 2000 years ago, and we impose our own values all too easily, but there are still voices who will say, 'Isn't that just typical? It reminds me of last Christmas when the whole lot of them were watching TV while I . . .'

Life is incredibly busy for many of us, and often there seems to be little we can do about it if we are to feed, clothe and shelter ourselves and those in our care. We want a busyness blessing. We want to be able to do the essential tasks with peace of mind, not in a state of stress or feeling that we are less worthy than our sisters and brothers who somehow have more time for prayer. But being so stressed and so busy can make us hasty in the way we hear things. Going back to the story of Martha and Mary, we might find a key to helping ourselves in the word 'choice'.

Mary and Martha are both under social pressure to be hospitable to honoured guests. Martha believes she has no choice but to conform to this pressure and work hard. Mary believes she has a choice not to conform, and downs tools. She is clearly not a slave to convention. Perhaps this is what is annoying Martha: she sees her sister claiming freedom, while she herself feels oppressed.

It is worth examining our own busyness and asking ourselves why we are doing what we are doing. Which parts are essential to survival? Which parts are because we like to feel needed, important, helpful, or to appear competent, dutiful, generous? Perhaps, on examination, there are areas where we are making choices about our lifestyle which take us, subtly, away from closeness to God for some reason. Perhaps we are filling our time because we are afraid of the conversation that might take place if we stop. Perhaps we don't want to hear what God has to say.

But this is not always the case. Not everybody is running away from God in their busyness. We may feel, like Martha, that we cannot willingly give our time and effort in loving service – 'prayer in action' – because we are being exploited. The answer, I think, is not the glib 'always serve humbly and willingly' which can be a route to complete exhaustion and the excuse many have used to keep subordinates submissive (a particular problem for women and slaves over the centuries). The answer comes from the Hebrew Scriptures. The real expression of one who knows they are exploited is to cry out to God – not a whining, self-pitying 'Oh poor me', but a real, deep outcry from the heart. When life enslaves us – and modern life does, in many ways – the response is to turn to God and ask for help.

In the Book of Exodus, we read about the huge effort that was required to free a whole people from slavery. It began with a cry – the cry of the oppressed – which God heard.

> Then the Lord said, 'I have observed the misery of my people who are in Egypt; I have heard their cry on account of their taskmasters. Indeed, I know their sufferings, and I have come down to deliver them.
>
> *Exodus 3:7, 8*

The one freedom we must have is to be able to walk with God in our daily life, busy or not. When we realise that this is what we want, too, and ask for help, what happens next is up to God. We may find that our spiritual liberation is a bigger and more challenging project than we had anticipated, and we may be tempted to go back to our life of disempowerment. But that is our choice.

Prayer of a found sheep

Eternal One, come to me in the glorious beauty of your self-giving, and ignite my love for you; call me by name to awaken my heart so that I want to spend my days with you. Set me free to worship you without fear. Forgetful of you, I lose my peace, so touch me and remind me of your love, day by day and hour by hour, in all that I do. Delight me, move me, so that my mind, my heart, my whole being become filled with the thought of you. Let me feel truly alive and free to walk with you wherever you lead me.

Amen.

SIX

Relating to the rest of the flock – an introduction followed by six reflections

Belonging to a flock

How does the sheep in Jesus' parable get lost in the first place? Did she or he just wander off? Did predators scatter the flock? Was she sick and fell behind? Or was there a problem with some of the other sheep? Did the other sheep notice and care?

Through applying our imagination (at the risk of anthropomorphising the sheep), we can see a lot about ourselves, our experiences and our views in the way we answer such questions. Exploring issues about belonging and not belonging, feeling welcome or excluded, can bring up a lot of feelings.

Naturally, we belong to many different groups during our lives, our family being the primal one, and in each group we experience different dynamics. Challenging relationships happen simply because we are collections of flawed human beings. I do not pretend to be an expert in relationships; I am simply making some observations from my own experiences of numerous churches and other groups over the past thirty years or so, sometimes feeling rather like a lost sheep and at other times taking on a degree of pastoral responsibility towards others.

In the reflections that follow, I have tended to focus on dynamics within church, but the issues are often transferable to the wider world. Relationships are relationships. The

Church, I think, has a hard job. We are faced, for a start, with
the precedent set by the earliest, Spirit-filled followers of
Jesus. Accounts in the New Testament about the beginnings
of the Church can leave us quite awed, and asking, 'What
have we lost?'

> All who believed were together and had all things in
> common; they would sell their possessions and goods
> and distribute the proceeds to all, as any had need. Day
> by day, as they spent much time together in the temple,
> they broke bread at home and ate their food with glad
> and generous hearts, praising God and having the
> goodwill of all the people. And day by day the Lord
> added to their number those who were being saved.
>
> *Acts 2:44-47*

In addition, as we know very well, Jesus gave us a particular
instruction, as recorded in John's Gospel:

> I give you a new commandment, that you love one
> another. Just as I have loved you, you also should love
> one another. By this everyone will know that you are
> my disciples, if you have love for one another.
>
> *John 13:34, 35*

Although we have been trying for the last 2000 years, we are
still finding that this is nigh impossible to achieve.
Admittedly, some churches are very caring, holy places to
be, and many Christians are very loving people. But as a
whole body, as well as all the good that has been done, if we
are honest, we have spent a great deal of time living out the
shadow side of our identity, not as lovers but as people
who feel unloved and unable to express love. It might have
been easier if the Gospel had said, 'I give you a new

commandment, that you *try* to love one another . . .' Perhaps then we would carry less of a sense of failure.

Earlier in the book we looked at 1 Corinthians 13 as a helpful unpacking of what it is to love.

> Love is patient; love is kind; love is not envious or boastful or arrogant or rude. It does not insist on its own way; it is not irritable or resentful; it does not rejoice in wrongdoing, but rejoices in the truth. It bears all things, believes all things, hopes all things, endures all things. *1 Corinthians 13:4-7*

Getting used to the idea that God might behave something like this towards us is one thing, but managing to be like this ourselves, even towards people we enjoy being with, is a lifetime's work. It takes a quite remarkable person to exhibit such qualities all the time, towards everybody they meet.

In education, there is a much-used phrase, 'working towards', which politely and positively describes the student's next learning target. Implicit in the statement is that they have not got there yet. We are, on the whole, working towards loving one another as Jesus would like us to. That, I believe, is accepted and understood by God our Shepherd, who knows that we are not perfect.

There is an element of denial sometimes, as churches and individual Christians try to brush the brokenness under the rug and look perfect in some moral or spiritual sense. Similarly, people can set out to look for a church that will meet all their needs and present a flawless embodiment of Christ at work in the world, only to be horribly disillusioned. Certainly, there is a need for us to act in a responsible rather than an antisocial manner and to aspire to live by the highest ideals and principles of our day, whatever we understand them to be, but beyond that, there is no perfect Christian and no single Christian viewpoint on what moral or spiritual perfection might be. There is not even agreement about what a perfect Christian might be like: even looking at Jesus (who was Jewish, not Christian!), we each see differently, from our own perspective. It depends what is already in our hearts.

It is whether we manage to love one another despite our differences that shows what is really in our hearts. Once we have mastered this within the 'safe' space of our churches, perhaps we will be able to live with the same respect in the wider world, where differences are even more marked. The question is whether church really is 'safe space' for everybody. Some people, it has to be said, do not feel safe, and one response is to leave. Another response is to hide their true selves away so nobody really knows them – but it can be difficult to be open with God when we cannot be honest about who we really are to other people. Another response is to become aggressive and attack what is causing the hurt – but the church is a big old body to strive against.

Not all church members, it has to be said, want the church to be a safe space for all comers. They want it to be a club for the 'in crowd'. People who do not conform to their rules of acceptability may find they are not completely welcome. To some degree this is perhaps human nature, but that does not excuse it. We are increasingly waking up to the fact that to the outside world it often seems that exclusivism based on subjective judgements is what church is all about – and this is a great cause for concern. We need, more than ever, to make it clear to this broken, complicated world that we, the body of Christ, are about love, and when we or somebody else get love wrong, then we are also about humility, forgiveness, peace, mercy, patience, and a striving towards wisdom – otherwise we are not the body of Christ. To give

God to others, we need to be able to offer refuge, access to the 'true pasture' which can nourish and restore.

Although we often struggle, we are bound by a beautiful vision. The biblical vision of hope, in both the New and the Old Testament, is of a time when all will live in harmony and peace. Impossible though it sounds, we dare to believe that through God's loving power, a place of peace will be established, in which not even predatory animals will need or want to kill any more. Our inner longing is for deep, genuine, complete peace, an end to all violence – even the violence of our own hearts.

> They will not hurt or destroy
> on all my holy mountain;
> for the earth will be full of the knowledge of the Lord
> as the waters cover the sea.   *Isaiah 11:9*

Christianity aims to follow Jesus who, in his temptation, ministry and death, refused to exercise earthly power, putting himself at the bottom of the pile, not the top. He came from among a subject, oppressed people, a flock at the mercy of cruel Roman shepherds, interested only in their own gain, who forced the rightful shepherds of Israel into compliance on pain of destruction. He stepped out from the midst of his flock and gave his own life for the sake of the others – the lamb who died, a willing sacrifice.

Try as we might to follow Jesus, how hard it is to live by his astonishing, reckless gentleness, his self-abandonment for love! Almost always, the best we can do is to recognise our own involvement in the dance of power and self-preservation, admit our own inner eruptions of anger, intolerance, hatred and bitterness, repent and consciously try to minimise the effect of this turmoil on other living things.

But we so easily knock each other's unhealed hurts, tread clumsily instead of lightly, misunderstand one another, judge harshly, act out of ignorance or selfishness, say too much and listen poorly – or we dare to disagree or cause offence because of who we are. Of course we do: we are human beings, each with our own limitations, needs and foibles. Recognising this corporate brokenness, gently and humbly, is part of loving one another, and it is a challenge.

Churches shelter great numbers of vulnerable and damaged people. They also contain many who are searching for meaning and asking difficult questions, along with a significant number with a mistaken belief in their own righteousness – or at least rightness – and their own agendas for having a bit of control over a little corner of existence. This is not an obvious recipe for harmony!

According to the writer of Matthew's Gospel, Jesus knew we would get in a mess, and told us what to do about it:

> Then Peter came and said to him, 'Lord, if another member of the church sins against me, how often should I forgive? As many as seven times?' Jesus said to him, 'Not seven times, but, I tell you, seventy-seven times.
> *Matthew 18:21, 22*

Forgiveness, too, can be very difficult – especially when we are sure that we are in the right and the other person is in the wrong! But when we feel unloved by people who are supposed to be loving us, and feel unforgiven by people who are supposed to be forgiving us, then it is understandable if we drift away. But if we become too distant from the flock, it can diminish our relationship with God; without meaning to, we lose touch. For what does a Christian community exist but to carry the gospel and the sacraments, to witness to Christ in the world, to nourish, guide, support, love, care and be the good soil where faith can grow and bear fruit?

What happens to a person's faith without this nourishment, support and immersion in Scripture? Can we survive as spiritual beings in love with God without this community life? This is an increasingly relevant question as we see numbers in our churches dwindling, year by year. There are many in society today who would claim to believe but who have no wish to set foot in a church. It is humbling and saddening to listen to some of the reasons people give for their choice.

All our struggles to get along with one another are part of the great journey each of us makes, of walking with Christ and learning about the love of God. We discover what love is, and what it is not. We see where love is, and where it is not. We see the outer world, trying to make sense of those we meet along the way and our relationship with them, and we see the inner world of our own hearts. When we are at a loss to find God anywhere 'out there' at all, we are reminded that there is one last place to look – deep within. For we are God's home. God is with us and deep within us; there is nowhere we can go that is outside of God's love.

For reflection
In the Gospels, Jesus spends time with all sorts of different people – disciples, religious scholars, crowds of villagers, crowds of city dwellers, sick people, parents and children . . . Sometimes he speaks as though he is identifying himself as the Shepherd.

> Do not be afraid, little flock, for it is your Father's good pleasure to give you the kingdom. *Luke 12:32*

How we view the 'flock' depends on who we are. Are we a leader, one of the crowd, a permanent fixture, a newcomer, somebody on the edge, somebody going through life changes, somebody needing support, somebody trying to make changes, somebody hoping to get noticed, somebody wanting some peace and quiet? Of course, we take different roles at different times. But whoever we are, the way we relate to the rest of the flock matters a great deal.

- What 'flocks', religious and otherwise, do you belong to at present, and have you belonged to in your past?
- What roles have you played in these flocks?
- Where is – and was – there love? And where is/was there difficulty in expressing and experiencing love?
- When there has been a need for forgiveness – by you and of you – how easy was this to achieve?
- When you have left 'flocks', what caused you to go?

Themed reflections about relating to the flock

The reflections in this chapter follow the same pattern as in the previous one. Again, there are six themes, and they are suitable for private reflection. In situations where a fully supportive and trusting environment can be created, they may also be suitable for group work. Please refer to the introduction to Chapter 5: Relating to God, for comments on the format and suggestions for use with a group.

Because the issues relate to personal experience, difficult feelings may arise. Please consider talking with somebody you trust, or seeking further help, if there are issues that trouble you.

1. Unanswered prayers for healing

Overview

We need to remember that healings happen in the Old Testament as well as the New, often through the prayers and works of inspiring figures such as Elijah the prophet.

According to the epistles, the ability to heal is a gift of the Holy Spirit. We find many instances of healing in the New Testament, by Jesus and the apostles, and also advice to pray with faith in order to receive what we request.

People in churches often pray for healing for one another. Experience tells us, however, that quite simply, many people pray in faith and remain ill. This can lead to feelings of failure and doubt – is our faith too weak? Is God against us? Instead of finding our faith built up by a miracle, we risk losing our faith out of disappointment and disillusionment, whether we are the one who has prayed or the one who is ill. Perhaps this has happened to you or somebody you know.

God wants us to live in loving trust whatever happens to us. Rather like a marriage, our relationship with God is meant to endure 'in sickness and in health'. We can actually hurt ourselves or vulnerable people in our community if we shift our trust away from simple obedience to God towards over-attachment to a particular outcome. The most important issue is our relationship with God and feeling able to walk with God through shadowy valleys as well as green pastures. When we are in a deepening love relationship with God, the meaning of 'healing' and 'wholeness' sometimes changes in unexpected ways.

Prayer of a lost sheep

They prayed for me.
They said they loved me.
They said Jesus loved me too,
and that he would help me
if only I would believe.
I believed but I wasn't healed.
Then they said my faith was too weak,
my love not strong enough,
and I had only myself to blame.

Then they gave me the cold shoulder
because my unhealed presence looked bad.
It flagged up failure within the group:
their failure, God's failure (heaven forbid),
all dismissed as *my* failure.

Encountering the Shepherd

In 2 Corinthians 12:7-10, Paul tells us something very helpful about himself.

> Therefore, to keep me from being too elated, a thorn was given to me in the flesh, a messenger of Satan to torment me, to keep me from being too elated. Three times I appealed to the Lord about this, that it would leave me, but he said to me, 'My grace is sufficient for you, for power is made perfect in weakness.' So, I will boast all the more gladly of my weaknesses, so that the power of Christ may dwell in me. Therefore I am content with weaknesses, insults, hardships, persecutions, and calamities for the sake of Christ; for whenever I am weak, then I am strong.

What was that thorn in Paul's flesh? Some say he was crippled or had a visual impairment; others claim he had malaria or even cancer. In truth, nobody knows. What we do know is that Paul, this great evangelist, uniquely gifted with a vision of the risen Christ, suffered an illness. He prayed not just once but three times for healing, but was not healed. What does he obtain from the experience? Does he lose faith? Does he rage at God? Does he blame the friends who also prayed for him? No, he gains an insight which he shares in order to help us. He says that the Lord tells him, 'My grace is sufficient for you, for power is made perfect in weakness.'

What does this statement say to you: 'My grace is sufficient for you, for power is made perfect in weakness'?

Paul then says, 'I will boast all the more gladly of my weaknesses, so that the power of Christ may dwell in me.'

Christ dwells in you – as in Paul – in your present situation. He does not wait for your perfection. He accepts your brokenness as his home. What does it mean to you, that Christ dwells in you?

Convinced of Christ's indwelling presence, Paul's faith is not crushed but strengthened, as he reaches a conclusion from which we can draw inspiration:

> Therefore I am content with weaknesses, insults, hardships, persecutions, and calamities for the sake of Christ; for whenever I am weak, then I am strong.

Let your mind linger over these words:

- I am content . . .
- I am content with hardships for the sake of Christ . . .
- . . . for whenever I am weak, then I am strong.
- How do these words make you feel? How do they relate to your own experience? Do they demand strength of you, or do they give you strength?

Prayers of a found sheep

Oh my Shepherd, I hand my whole being over to you: body, mind and spirit. You know my pain, my brokenness and the fears that trouble me. You know my disappointments and you also know what is best for me, beyond my own understanding. Help me to accept myself lovingly as you do, and to take care of myself. Help me to calm my mind. Make your home in me, O God, and use my weakness as strength. Always let me journey with you, and deepen my trust so that I, like Paul, can learn to be content in you.

Amen.

Oh my Shepherd, help me to give appropriate loving care to people who turn to me. Help me to understand that there is more to prayer, more to healing, more to you than I can ever understand. Help me to accept that your way is often subtle, quiet and gentle and asks patience and humility of us. Help me to accept that it may not be through my prayers that a person will find joy, but by seeking refuge in you. And help me to accept that we do not know your unfathomable mind but can only trust in your goodness and mercy, your knowledge of us and your presence with us now and always.

Amen.

Note: If you are experiencing distress due to physical or mental sickness, you might find support in my book, *Hiding in God: Reflecting on personal health concerns through prayer*, (Kevin Mayhew 2012).

2. Acceptance and rejection

Overview

Some of us experience rejection by other Christians because we are seen to be outside the acceptable norm in some way. For many churches this can be about sexuality. Many who identify themselves as gay, lesbian, bisexual or transgender have heartbreaking stories to tell of judgement and rejection at the hands of church communities which they would like to belong to, if only they were made to feel welcome and equal. Other churches may have (sometimes unspoken) issues regarding political allegiance; others struggle with past history, outside interests, economic status, and so on. Perhaps you have come across other reasons.

Questions about inclusion and exclusion within the Church go right back to its early days as communities wrestled with issues of forgiveness, ethical standards, responsibilities and accountability – the very identity of the movement itself – desperately aware that a hostile world was looking in at this fragile group and making its own judgements.

The world still looks on, and what does it see? How do we seem to be defining ourselves? Are we a movement struggling to maintain our integrity and hold on to the sanctity of holy living against all odds? Or do we come across as some out-of-date institution, a last bastion of what should be obsolete, even antisocial, values?

How do we learn to work with our differences and reflect humbly on our own positions, daring to ask whether it really is 'the other' who needs to change, or ourselves? And how do we give and receive genuine compassion and respect to all, as we seek to reflect Christ's love with integrity? How do we show the world what loving community really means? And does the world 'out there' sometimes challenge us in rethinking what loving one's neighbour really means?

Prayer of a lost sheep

I thought Christians were good at compassion and gentleness, so I came to church
expecting to find people who were willing to accept me just as I am
and try to understand me.
But instead I found people making assumptions about me
and rejecting things about me, who I am.
They wanted to change me into someone
that it felt safe to love.
They wanted to remould me
into something acceptable to them.
They are telling me I am not acceptable to God.

But God made me the way I am –
if God wants that to change,
surely God will change me?
Is it not their place simply to love me
and accept my right to worship God
in peace and fellowship
and without fear?

Encountering the Shepherd

When we think and pray about issues of inclusion and
exclusion, it can be challenging but also helpful to remember
that Jesus himself is described as suffering rejection. Trying
to make sense of Jesus' death, his followers turned to the
Hebrew Scriptures and found passages such as Isaiah 53:3:

He was despised and rejected by others;
a man of suffering and acquainted with infirmity;
and as one from whom others hide their faces
he was despised, and we held him of no account.

and Psalm 118:22:

The stone that the builders rejected
has become the chief cornerstone.

That is, the rejected one is discovered to be of value. When
we are tempted to exclude and reject people, for whatever
reason, we need to ask ourselves a question: do we risk
casting someone away who, in God's eyes, is valuable?
What is the yardstick we use to decide what is acceptable
and what is unacceptable? Or can we – should we – find a
way to accept all, unconditionally?

From the other perspective, when we feel rejected, I think
we can find refuge in the same psalm:

Let those who fear the Lord say,
'His steadfast love endures for ever.'
Out of my distress I called on the Lord;
the Lord answered me and set me in a broad place.
With the Lord on my side I do not fear.
What can mortals do to me?
The Lord is on my side to help me;
I shall look in triumph on those who hate me.
It is better to take refuge in the Lord
than to put confidence in mortals.   *Psalm 118:4-8*

The primary relationship for every single person is with God. Each person is accountable to God and is invited to ask themselves whether they are living with integrity, and whether they can really flee to the divine embrace for refuge. God knows our hearts; God made us. God wants from us, not perfection, but loving devotion. If we endure loneliness, if we feel cut off from others, we are not alone in the history of our faith, and we are not alone spiritually.

Prayers of a found sheep

Oh my Shepherd, thank you for lifting me up and showing me a wider perspective, for helping me to see beyond my own issues to the greater call to become more loving, more forgiving and more compassionate, as I seek to follow you faithfully. Before I condemn others, teach me to look at myself. Before I criticise or ostracise, test my heart and see if there is any unkindness in me – a spirit of bitterness or a lack of generosity, a desire to control or a refusal to accept the other for who they are and value them as your child. Change me, O God, and open my heart, lest I condemn the innocent or create a stumbling block in another's path to you.

Amen.

141

Oh my Shepherd, thank you for loving me just as I am, and showing me that I matter to you, that your message is for me, that you reach out to me without demanding that I change before you can accept me. I just need to know that I am held and am precious in your eyes, and from that safe place I can start to feel stronger. With you, I can become the person you created me to be, alive in your Spirit and made beautiful within, by your grace.

Amen.

3. 'Rescuing'

Overview

Many are drawn to churches, feeling that there will be people there who will give them the support they need. Looking after one another, looking out for one another's physical, emotional and spiritual well-being is part of loving one another. But how do we do that well, deeply, genuinely? When we see someone who appears to be struggling, what do we do? When we are the person who is struggling, what would we like others to do? Will 'helping' seem like interference? Are opportunities for kindness being missed? This is an area where it is painfully easy to hurt where we mean to help, and to be hurt when no harm was meant at all.

How do we discern the difference between real help that makes a difference to a person's peace of mind and the kinds of 'helping' that come from unspoken desires to control, to be seen to be doing good, to be needed, or even to keep people dependent on or obedient to the church? How can we truly empower others to journey in the confidence of Christ, and strive for that empowerment in our own lives?

Prayer of a lost sheep

I know they mean well,
but they really don't understand
and their interference is making things worse.
They think they can see what the problem is,
but how can they,
unless they can see right into my heart and soul –
like you can, Holy One.
I feel as though you are leading me one way
but they are trying to drag me another.
They seem to think I should just follow blindly,
or let them carry me and do all my thinking for me,
but they are not allowing for the fact
that you may be at work in my life already in ways they
cannot see.
They are not helping me to walk with you.
Do I really have to choose
between staying with them
and following what I believe is your voice?

Encountering the Shepherd

Humans are resourceful, emotionally intelligent and capable
of great courage, strength, insight, humour and more. The
shepherd's role as a good pastor of humans is to notice such
qualities within us and to help us appreciate them and
understand how to use them to help ourselves.

In John 2:24, 25 we read that Jesus 'knew all people' and
'knew what was in everyone'. His knowing is the inner sight
of God. To be able to understand people is a divine quality.

Jesus also knows what is in all the people in your life and
beyond. He knows everyone. His knowing leads to works of
great compassion.

Jesus knew all of the people involved in an event that is described in the Gospels of Matthew, Mark and Luke – the healing of a person suffering from paralysis:

> Then some people came, bringing to him a paralysed man, carried by four of them. And when they could not bring him to Jesus because of the crowd, they removed the roof above him; and after having dug through it, they let down the mat on which the paralytic lay. When Jesus saw their faith, he said to the paralytic, 'Son, your sins are forgiven.' Now some of the scribes were sitting there, questioning in their hearts, 'Why does this fellow speak in this way? It is blasphemy! Who can forgive sins but God alone?' At once Jesus perceived in his spirit that they were discussing these questions among themselves; and he said to them, 'Why do you raise such questions in your hearts? Which is easier, to say to the paralytic, "Your sins are forgiven", or to say, "Stand up and take your mat and walk"? But so that you may know that the Son of Man has authority on earth to forgive sins' – he said to the paralytic – 'I say to you, stand up, take your mat and go to your home.' And he stood up, and immediately took the mat and went out before all of them; so that they were all amazed and glorified God, saying, 'We have never seen anything like this!' *Mark 2:3-12*

The focal characters are Jesus, a group of very determined friends and a man suffering from paralysis. The friends bring their companion to Jesus. Jesus appreciates their confidence in him. The man with paralysis is fortunate to have such good friends who want him to be free of this condition but who accept that they themselves cannot 'fix' him.

When we see someone we perceive to have a problem, how do we decide what is right for them? At what point do we involve God in our efforts? At what point do we involve the other person?

Jesus, who knows all people, understands what has 'bound' this person and speaks the right words to set him free. Jesus ignores his critics and, without extracting a confession or statement of repentance, tells the sufferer that his sins are forgiven.

What space do we give people to explore their feelings and unburden themselves before God? How readily and gently are the channels of reconciliation offered as paths to healing? What hurdles do we put up between people and the message of forgiveness?

Jesus says one more thing, through which he shifts the person from dependence on others into a new state in which he is empowered to help himself. Jesus says, 'Stand up, take your mat and go to your home.'

If we really want to help a person, how can we help them to become truly free to walk wherever they choose?

How easy is it for us to be like those good friends, to bring another to the point where they no longer need us?

In our own difficulties, do we *want* to be able to help ourselves, or do we actually like being carried by our companions?

Prayers of a found sheep

My Shepherd, give me wisdom so that I can support people in a way that helps them become more fully themselves. Teach me to understand what it is that is really needed, and then guide me in meeting that need. Help me to lay aside my own opinions, my desire to rush in and rescue, my haste to problem solve. Give me patience, that I may pause long enough to ask where your love lies, and in what way you are already present. Open me to serve you humbly, according to your will, O God, rather than my own.

Amen.

My Shepherd, thank you for being the one who understands me. Thank you that, even when I feel pushed around by others, my private life intruded upon, there is always a deep, secret place in my heart which only you know – a safe place where I can retreat into your love. Strengthen me, O God, so that I can help myself. Embolden me and give me the confidence in you that leads to peace. Give me the grace to forgive those who intrude, accepting that they mean well, but give me also a sense of freedom, so that I can follow you freely.

Amen.

4. Being heard

Overview

Within a group, every single member matters. Scripture reassures us of this – for example, the Epistle of James (James 2:1-8) reminds members to value the poor as highly as the wealthy. In Acts 6:1-6, we read of strategies put in place to make sure food distribution is fair. Paul talks about each person making up part of a body – their uniqueness adding to the whole (1 Corinthians 12:12-26). Jesus talks about becoming the least in order to be greatest in God's eyes (Mark 9:33-35).

The laws and prophetic utterances of the Hebrew Scriptures again and again tell us that the needs of the least in a community must be met. So within church, our voice matters, our feelings matter, our ideas and questions matter, our perception of justice and injustice matter, whoever we are. With all the time and energy that are devoted to teaching and preaching, administrating and fund-raising, what time is given to really listening to one another? What credit are we really given for being able to raise a concern or express an opinion? We need to be heard, and our voice valued.

A great deal can be gained by this listening, for the hearer and the person speaking, in terms of deepening respect and mutual understanding. Without this sense that somebody is genuinely interested in us and our perspective, we can start to feel that we are not considered important – and we can wander off.

Prayer of a lost sheep

I come week after week.
I sit here, I sing, I pray, I listen,
I give my money, I do my bit,
but what I'd really like is for someone to spend time with me
and ask me what I really care about –
what troubles me,
what I'd long to learn more about,
what I have learned through my own walk with God.
But they don't ask, so they don't know,
and the feeling that I'm not known,
my walk not witnessed,
makes me feel that I'm not valued,
and if I'm not valued,
why do I come here,
add my name to the rotas
and my money to the collection plate
week after week?

Encountering the Shepherd

In Exodus 18 we read of Moses in the wilderness with the Hebrew people. Jethro, Moses' father-in-law and priest of Midian, visits the encampment, bringing Moses' wife Zipporah and their two sons with him. Jethro is a wise elder. He watches Moses at work for a day, as he deals with case after case that is brought to him by the people. At the end of the day, he advises Moses that he will exhaust himself. Two things are needed. First, the people need to be better informed so they can make more decisions for themselves:

> Teach them the statutes and instructions and make known to them the way they are to go and the things they are to do. *Exodus 18:20*

Then, from among the people, respected individuals need to be designated who can listen to concerns group by group:

> Let them sit as judges for the people at all times; let them bring every important case to you, but decide every minor case themselves. So it will be easier for you, and they will bear the burden with you. If you do this, and God so commands you, then you will be able to endure, and all these people will go to their home in peace. *Exodus 18:22, 23*

(A judge, by the way, in the early days of the Israelites, was a wider term than it is today; it was not simply a legal executor of justice. A judge was a father or a mother to the people who would give advice, even speak prophetically, and rise up to lead the people in time of trouble – see characters such as Deborah and Gideon in the Book of Judges.)

So, says Jethro, a team of listeners needs to be established in order that every case is heard. From a management perspective, this is sound advice on reducing workload. But from the perspective of the people, it is even better: they don't need to waste a day queuing to spend a few minutes with one key figure who may not even know their name. They can talk to somebody nearby who is more on their level, who does know them, and who has the sole job of taking an interest.

This becomes a primary structure amongst the Hebrew people – they are a people with a voice, and each person has somebody they can trust to take up their case and understand their situation. How might it feel to belong to such a support network as this?

At the end of verse 23 above, Jethro emphasises the point of creating this structure: 'all these people will go to their home in peace.'

What can we do for one another that will allow us to go to our homes in peace?

Paul gives words of advice to the Colossians concerning this peace, which as Christians we have come to know in that most beautiful gift – the peace of Christ. It is a peace that rules the hearts of those who live in the spirit of God's love, as the true Church:

> As God's chosen ones, holy and beloved, clothe yourselves with compassion, kindness, humility, meekness, and patience. Bear with one another and, if anyone has a complaint against another, forgive each other; just as the Lord has forgiven you, so you also must forgive. Above all, clothe yourselves with love, which binds everything together in perfect harmony. And let the peace of Christ rule in your hearts, to which indeed you were called in the one body. And be thankful. *Colossians 3:12-15*

Prayers of a found sheep

Oh my Shepherd, help me to listen well, to take the time to really hear what people are telling me about their own lives. Remind me, when I get too busy, that it is people who make up the Church, it is the people who matter, and who need your patience and compassion. So let me become someone that people can trust with their concerns, knowing they will be respected.

Amen.

Oh my Shepherd, help me to find someone I can trust to talk to, who will listen without judging me and make me feel that I matter. Help me to find a person who is wise and kind, who will understand but not try to interfere or take over the conversation with their own agenda. Give me the confidence, O God, to raise my concerns, so that I can resolve them and be able to move on. In the meantime, help me to bring my burdens to you, knowing that you will lift them from me.

Amen.

5. Feeling let down

Overview

We all have needs – physical, mental, emotional and spiritual – and from childhood we look to other people to meet them. This mutual care is part of what community and family are about. Unfortunately, sometimes our expectations of other people do not match what they can deliver. This can make us feel angry or let down. From the other point of view, we can sometimes feel that someone is asking too much of us, or asking something we cannot give.

Human nature means we fail sometimes, and that includes letting others down, even without realising it.

The Bible tells us that God is the only one we can fully depend on. God is our true security, our rock, our unfailing love. This doesn't mean that we can give up on people, and can just sit and wait for God to do something, or abdicate responsibilities; it means living in hope. Living hopefully, living with an expectation that all will be well because of God's presence in our lives, is part of living faithfully.

Prayer of a lost sheep

They have really let me down.
I thought I could rely on them,
and they knew I was waiting for them to help,
but what happened?
Nothing.
Have they no idea how I'm feeling?
Can't they see how difficult my life is?
Isn't a church a place where people do good to one another?
Well, I think I came to the wrong place;
it's all very well talking about love,
but when it comes down to practicalities,
it seems nobody really wants to follow through.
So now what am I supposed to do?
Just turn up as usual as though nothing has happened?
Well, I'm not sure I want to any more.
Besides, they might be quite glad if I left,
since I'm obviously asking too much.

Encountering the Shepherd

Jesus knows we become frustrated with one another sometimes. He, of all people, was let down by his own disciples the night he was arrested. While he was praying in the Garden of Gethsemane, what did he ask them to do?

> I am deeply grieved, even to death; remain here, and stay awake with me.   *Matthew 26:38*

And what did they do? They fell asleep, not just once, but three times.

Earlier that evening, when Jesus had explained what was going to happen, Peter in particular said, 'Though all become deserters because of you, I will never desert you' (Matthew 26:33). But what does he do? Once Jesus is arrested, Peter denies that he even knows him (Matthew 26:69-75).

Jesus knows about being let down.

But Jesus also understands the weakness of human nature; he knows exactly what will happen when he is arrested and uses a passage of Scripture (Zechariah 13:7) to warn them:

> It is written, 'I will strike the shepherd,
> and the sheep of the flock will be scattered.'
>
> *Matthew 26:31*

He does not waste time with the disciples working out how they can support him in his last hours; he simply turns to God in prayer, sad that they cannot even stay awake to pray with him, but surely not surprised.

Following the resurrection, when his followers experience the risen Christ, what does he say? Is he full of recriminations against these people who have failed him? Is there a trace of bitterness in his words? According to John's Gospel, the risen Jesus entered the room where they were hiding:

> Jesus came and stood among them and said, 'Peace be with you.' *John 20:19*

We cannot pretend to be any better than these disciples. In our moments of failure, and at the times we feel let down ourselves, our hope is in Jesus' forgiving words, 'Peace be with you.'

What does this mean for you?

Prayer of a found sheep

Oh my Shepherd, what can I say except 'thank you' and 'I am sorry'? I am sorry because I realise my own weaknesses and I know I am only as human as your disciples all that time ago, who failed you but whom you still greeted with peace. And I am sorry because I know there are times when I let others down; I pray that they can forgive me, just as you teach me to forgive those who let me down.

Thank you for your presence, that you are with me and know my needs. Thank you that even before I ask, you understand and delight that my heart has turned to you. Help me, O God, and strengthen my trust in you, so that I can pray in faith, knowing that you love me.

Amen.

6. Pressure, being burdened

Overview

A church community usually has ideas about its survival and asks certain things of people who belong to the group. This is likely to include a financial contribution, but it may also include gifts of time, expertise, the sharing of belongings or home, and more. The vision of the embryonic church in the period after Pentecost shows a group of people who were completely committed to giving their all, with joy, and this is an ideal we hold on to. In the Book of Acts, we read how this gradually changed as people struggled with exactly how much they were prepared to give.

Once we have decided we want to be part of a group, we know we are entering into a reciprocal relationship – we will give and receive. From the start, we are already bringing something very valuable: ourselves. We have intrinsic worth. Anything on top of the basic gathering of people for worship and reflection is a bonus and depends on the priorities of a gathering. We try to build up our communities in ways that address the needs that present themselves and the resources available. This is all well and good, until somebody starts to feel exploited, taken for granted or pressurised – guilt tripped. Once such feelings arise, we have to ask ourselves whether 'worldly' ways of getting things done are supplanting 'kingdom' ways. If work is done under duress, rather than for love, is it really church?

Prayer of a lost sheep
I think I'm being used.
Of course I want to give,
but I would like some say in what I give,
without being pressurised
into doing what I don't enjoy.
Saying something makes it sound as though
I've got a bad attitude
or I want a free ride.
But it's not that;
I just want to give what I want to give,
not this.

Encountering the Shepherd
Paul gives the believers in Galatia some advice about community living:

> My friends, if anyone is detected in a transgression, you who have received the Spirit should restore such a one in a spirit of gentleness. Take care that you yourselves are not tempted. Bear one another's burdens, and in

this way you will fulfil the law of Christ. For if those who are nothing think they are something, they deceive themselves. All must test their own work; then that work, rather than their neighbour's work, will become a cause for pride. For all must carry their own loads . . .

So let us not grow weary in doing what is right, for we will reap at harvest time, if we do not give up. So then, whenever we have an opportunity, let us work for the good of all, and especially for those of the family of faith. *Galatians 6:1-5, 9, 10*

Notice how lovingly he begins, in the spirit of the true Shepherd who seeks the recovery of every lost sheep:

If anyone is detected in a transgression, you who have received the Spirit should restore such a one in a spirit of gentleness.

Jesus himself told Peter that we should never tire of this restoration of those who go astray – 'seventy-seven times', or 'seventy times seven', we are to forgive (Matthew 18:22). This is worth remembering, not only by those in the weaker position who feel they have been put upon, but those in the stronger position too, when people refuse to help, walk away, down tools, make excuses or become confrontational. There is a reason for the lack of cooperation, and this calls for reflection. By putting pressure on someone, are we causing them to sin in their attempt to extricate themselves?

Paul says that we should 'bear one another's burdens, and in this way you will fulfil the law of Christ.' It seems he is referring to a transgressor's burden – the heavy feelings that are bound up with the sense of lostness. I think he is asking us to support one another emotionally and spiritually with the things we struggle with in life. This

Christlike loving kindness is part of the process of restoration that helps a person not to stray too far from the Shepherd: their safety within the flock is affirmed, even if they are making mistakes.

This sense of safety allows a person to feel valued, not just because of their usefulness to the group but because of who they are. To be valued by God, nobody needs to *do* anything; we are simply God's children and we are loved. Such an environment also helps a person to explore what they really want to give and to say what they really think. This, as we know, leads to much more honest relationships.

Paul goes on to say that we need to 'test' or look at our own work rather than that of the next person; we need to be able to consider our contribution in the light of our own conscience. Each of us stands before God accountable for our own deeds, and in this sense we each carry our own load. We cannot bring somebody else's life-work to God. But God is all-knowing, merciful and full of grace, so despite the inadequacy of our offering, we are still valued as beloved children.

What we do, then, is first and foremost a matter between us and God. If what we do seems to be a way of serving God, we usually feel differently about it than if we were to feel it is a waste of time. In your own life, you may have many roles, some of which seem more of a burden than others; some of which are more of a joy than others.

Pause for a while to reflect on your activities and why you do each one.

Paul's last sentence in this quotation (verse 10) seems to be what he has been building up to. Having created this loving, safe environment, having reminded the members of the group that they each stand before God with their own efforts, having invited people to examine their own conscience, he now feels he can ask his readers to accept the

Christian calling to humble and loving service: 'let us work for the good of all'. There is nothing specific here. He does not give a list of jobs, from secretary to children's club facilitator to jumble-sale organiser to caretaker; he simply invites us to think about what 'for the good of all' means.

What does 'for the good of all' mean to you?

What does it mean for your church?

Prayers of a found sheep

Oh my Shepherd, I am sorry if I have placed a burden on others which adds to their troubles rather than giving them joy and helping to deepen their relationship with you. Help me to value people for themselves, not according to their usefulness, and help me to see the well-being of each one as a priority. As I organise and mobilise, give me a greater sense of trust in the Holy Spirit, alive and at work in our midst, so that I can let go my need to control and allow your presence to shine through. Help me to forgive those I feel are letting us down; help me to treat all with gentleness and work to create an environment where people feel safe to act and speak openly, and give of their best for love.

Amen.

Oh my Shepherd, thank you for offering to take my burdens from me. I bring them to you in prayer and lay them down, like so many sacks, at your feet. The freedom you offer is a blessing, and I delight in your love for me. Let this be the reason for my acts of service; let all that I do come from a desire to be close to you.

Amen.

SEVEN

Relating to self – an introduction followed by ten reflections

Can we love ourselves?

Many people say that one of the beauties of our faith is that we have a 'personal God' who knows us and loves us, and who we can relate to, person to person. The 'person' I have emphasised throughout this book is the figure of the Good Shepherd. Chapter 5 explored relating to this loving God, and chapter 6 explored our relationships with other people in our communities – our 'flock'. The fundamental relationship, however, which impacts on all other relationships, is our relationship with ourselves. Who are we? What do we think of ourselves? How do we describe ourselves to others? Are we able to love ourselves?

Being able to love ourselves matters very much. I described earlier how one day I suddenly found during the course of a bus ride across the city that I could look at my life with compassion instead of bitterness and self-criticism. Once I found I could be so forgiving with myself, for that wonderful twenty minutes or so, it transformed my way of seeing everybody else, too, and made me appreciate that God's compassion must be so much bigger than I had previously been able to even begin to imagine.

I think it works the other way too: when we are not able to love ourselves, we can also struggle to believe that God might love us. If we are sure we are unlovable, what will we do but hide from the presence of the divine? Encountering a God who does not love us is a frightening thought. Maybe it is better to believe in no God than an unloving one. Yet God *is* love and *does* value us, so Scripture tells us, and if God loves us and values us, then, as Julian of Norwich famously put it, 'all shall be well and all manner of things shall be well'.[1]

Loving ourselves does not mean excusing ourselves or spoiling ourselves; it is not about self-indulgence at all, but about self-awareness and a desire to grow into our God-given potential. It is about having a healthy concern for our own well-being, a self-respect that means we look after the body and mind God has given us, and seek after the wholesome rather than the harmful in the choices we make. Whatever shape it's in, our body is God's home; God dwells in us – even in our brokenness. False humility can make us conclude that because we are not worthy to be God's home, we should close ourselves off. This voluntary shutdown of relationship is a sign of our lostness, a lack of trust in God's grace. Even though we do not deserve it, we are promised God's merciful love. The parable of the lost sheep assures us that God does not give up on us when we hide away like this, but patiently and tenderly works towards our inner freedom and healing.

Matthew 10:16 describes Jesus both warning and reassuring his disciples as he sends them out to preach and heal. He tells them they will be going out like 'sheep into the midst of wolves', completely vulnerable, as though already marked for death. Indeed, many of Jesus' disciples met violent deaths in the course of time – yet in God their souls were safe whether they lived or died:

Are not two sparrows sold for a penny? Yet not one of them will fall to the ground unperceived by your

1. Julian of Norwich, *Revelations of Divine Love* (Penguin Books, 1998), page 22.

Father. And even the hairs of your head are all counted.
So do not be afraid; you are of more value than
many sparrows.   *Matthew 10:29-31*

We are of value to God. When we give of ourselves, we are
offering a precious gift in the eyes of God who treasures us.
Our self-giving is not the throwing away of a piece of
worthless rubbish; it is a profound act of love. It is natural to
want to preserve our own lives. Even Jesus in the Garden of
Gethsemane prayed that the 'cup' of his impending death
would be taken from him so that he could go on living and
loving (Matthew 26:39). He did not give himself up to death
lightly; neither do we make our own lesser sacrifices lightly,
day by day. They cost us. But when we *do* put love of others
ahead of self-interest, despite the love we have of our own
lives, then our giving is of God.

As well as the Good Shepherd, Jesus is also called the
Lamb of God – the lamb who died. The Temple sacrifices in
Jerusalem helped early Christians to make sense of Jesus'
death – it was not simply a meaningless, ugly killing but
rather an act which ultimately gave glory to God. Jesus'
innocence and gentleness were conveyed in the image of the
lamb, but unlike a domestic creature, he was not picked out
of the flock at random; he stepped up willingly.

For reflection

- In our own living, how do we learn to take on this
  gentleness and willingness to give of self for the
  greater good?
- If we believe Jesus was ready to die for us, what does
  that tell us of our value to God, and the power with
  which God loves us? Does this allow us to dare to
  love ourselves too, because God first loved us?

Who am I?

'Who am I?' is a question St Francis of Assisi often took to prayer: according to the medieval work, *The Little Flowers of St Francis*, he spent hours in deep devotion asking, 'Who art thou, my dearest Lord? And who am I . . . ?'[2] The question turns around into a statement: 'I am.' This could be the most important statement of all time because, as we read in Exodus 3:14, it is the revealed name of God – or an approximation of it. God's holy name is a statement of pure existence. In prayer, we, too, can sit with this notion and discover that we simply *'are'*: we can just 'be' for a little while, if only we can still our minds and rest our bodies. In such quietness, we become more open to the presence of God all around and within us; oneness with God somehow becomes more believable.

More often, in the course of our daily lives, we feel the need to add information to this statement of existence. We often make statements about ourselves that start with 'I am'. How many ways can we finish the statement? In a day, I might say, 'I am hungry', 'I am tired', 'I am sorry', 'I am fine', 'I am late' . . . I might include statements about my role or status: 'I am a mother, a wife, a teacher, a writer . . .'; it all depends on the context, and of course, what we say changes over time, as we change.

Sometimes our choice of words can limit us. If I say, 'I am left-handed,' it is understood that I am not right-handed. The statement goes some way towards classifying me, helping others to make sense of me, allowing me to get the most out of life. 'I am an artist' invites people to apportion poster-designing jobs and run craft tables at church fêtes. 'I

---

2. *The Little Flowers of St Francis*, chapter LIII, http://www.ewtn.com/library/mary/flowers1.htm. Accessed 4 February 2013.

am not good with figures,' warns the PCC to give the job of treasurer to somebody else.

What might you say about yourself?

Describing ourselves can be very necessary, but it can also sometimes mask deeper issues. We – and others – can start to believe our own summary of ourselves rather than the deeper truth that we are beloved children of God, sheep of the divine Shepherd. The way we talk about ourselves matters. Sometimes we big ourselves up, and sometimes we put ourselves down – but what is really true about us? Who are we really? We hardly know, we cannot fully understand, yet Scripture tells us that we are mortal and earthy, and blessed by God. In Psalm 8 we are reminded of this deeper truth:

When I look at your heavens, the work of your fingers,
the moon and the stars that you have established;
what are human beings that you are mindful of them,
mortals that you care for them?
Yet you have made them a little lower than God,
and crowned them with glory and honour.   *Psalm 8:3-5*

The Good Shepherd, calling us by name

One of the ways of finishing the statement 'I am . . .' is to give our name. Our name is an essential part of our identity. Any institution which substitutes numbers or other codes for people's names dehumanises them; it is a warning sign that they will have their uniqueness devalued in some way.

When we get lost, what gives us more joy than the sound of somebody we love, calling out our name? In the passage below, we read that the shepherd 'calls his own sheep by name and leads them out'.

> Very truly, I tell you, anyone who does not enter the
> sheepfold by the gate but climbs in by another way is a
> thief and a bandit. The one who enters by the gate is
> the shepherd of the sheep. The gatekeeper opens the
> gate for him, and the sheep hear his voice. He calls his
> own sheep by name and leads them out. When he has
> brought out all his own, he goes ahead of them, and the
> sheep follow him because they know his voice.

John 10:1-4

In the Hebrew Scriptures, God is often said to call people by
name. In Isaiah 43:1, for example, God says:

> Do not fear, for I have redeemed you;
> I have called you by name, you are mine.

God our Shepherd calls us by name. But what name does
God use? Perhaps it is the name our loved ones call us.
When Mary Magdalene is in the garden, mourning the
death of Jesus and wondering where his body has gone,
what is more powerful than the single word of love from the
risen Jesus: 'Mary'?

> Jesus said to her, 'Woman, why are you weeping? For
> whom are you looking?' Supposing him to be the
> gardener, she said to him, 'Sir, if you have carried him
> away, tell me where you have laid him, and I will take
> him away.' Jesus said to her, 'Mary!' She turned and said
> to him in Hebrew, 'Rabbouni!' (which means Teacher).

John 20:15, 16

We can imagine ourselves into this scene as we sit in our
own distress, with our own feelings of confusion, doubt,
sorrow and regret. Tears and suffering cloud our vision of

reality; yet it is Jesus who comes to us in our pain, Jesus who has suffered more than any, and who has been raised from the dead. It is Jesus who appears in the garden of our sorrow and speaks our most familiar name.

Again, in John's Gospel, when Jesus talks with Peter at the side of the lake, he calls him not by the nickname he gave him – Peter – but by the name his parents gave him – Simon. It is a serious moment of commissioning in which this disciple who has failed Jesus so badly is asked to put this behind him and step up, to grow into the potential that God sees in him:

Simon son of John, do you love me more than these?

John 21:15

The passage poignantly shows the transition Simon Peter makes, from a frightened sheep, scattering because of the loss of his shepherd, to the position of shepherd himself. It is not a role he can take on by himself; he needs the strength of Christ to empower him, because in the end he, too, will lay down his life for the sake of the sheep.

When they had finished breakfast, Jesus said to Simon Peter, 'Simon son of John, do you love me more than these?' He said to him, 'Yes, Lord; you know that I love you.' Jesus said to him, 'Feed my lambs.' A second time he said to him, 'Simon son of John, do you love me?' He said to him, 'Yes, Lord; you know that I love you.' Jesus said to him, 'Tend my sheep.' He said to him the third time, 'Simon son of John, do you love me?' Peter felt hurt because he said to him the third time, 'Do you love me?' And he said to him, 'Lord, you know everything; you know that I love you.' Jesus said to him, 'Feed my sheep. Very truly, I tell you, when you were younger, you used to fasten your own belt and to go wherever you wished. But when you grow old, you will stretch out your hands, and someone else will fasten a belt around you and take you where you do not wish to go.' (He said this to indicate the kind of death by which he would glorify God.) After this he said to him, 'Follow me.'   *John 21:15-19*

The meaning of names

Perhaps, sometimes, the Shepherd uses a new name that describes a quality or gift that God has given us and loves in us. When Jesus meets Simon, brother of Andrew, for the first time, he names him Peter, or Cephas, which as we know means 'rock'. People have enjoyed speculating on what he meant ever since, but most agree it reflects something of the disciple's nature, which Jesus saw. As with so many of Jesus' expressions, it is an image from nature.

If Jesus were to use an image from nature to capture your unique identity, what would it be? Are you on fire with passion? Do you flow through life like water? Are you daydreamy as the clouds, down to earth, strong as an ox, bright as a sunflower? How do you see yourself?

It is interesting that, in English-speaking cultures, we have become one step removed from the meaning of many of the names we use. We have names from Greek, Latin, French, Hebrew, Germanic, Anglo-Saxon, Gaelic and an increasing number of other roots – a testimony to our cultural diversity. But unless we are familiar with these languages, we do not necessarily know what a person's name means. The meaning of my name – Annie – for example, is not obvious at all, but passing through French and Greek we arrive at the Hebrew 'Hannah', which means 'grace', which was the name of one of my grandmothers.

Many other cultures, including biblical, draw on their living vocabulary so that the meaning of a name is obvious to all hearers: the name *is* the meaning. Many babies in the Bible are named for a reason, sometimes at God's command, including Jesus, whose name means 'God saves'. Thus in an English translation of Ruth 1:20, 21, Naomi, who is now widowed and bereft of her two adult sons, says:

> Call me no longer Naomi,
> call me Mara,
> for the Almighty has dealt bitterly with me.
> I went away full,
> but the Lord has brought me back empty;
> why call me Naomi
> when the Lord has dealt harshly with me,
> and the Almighty has brought calamity upon me?

To understand this passage, we need to know that 'Naomi' means 'pleasant', and 'Mara' means 'bitter'. So the woman is really saying, 'Don't call me Pleasant; call me Bitter.' Her identity and her experience are expressed in her name. According to biblical tradition, our name reflects something about ourselves; if it does not, then as with Peter, God might give us a new name. Take the following passage from Revelation 2:17:

> Let anyone who has an ear listen to what the Spirit is saying to the churches. To everyone who conquers I will give some of the hidden manna, and I will give a white stone, and on the white stone is written a new name that no one knows except the one who receives it.

This God-given name, I imagine, describes something about our very nature. What will it say? Will it be a quality we have developed, or a blessing we have received? Will it simply speak of God's love for us, despite our troubles? Has it been written since the beginning of time, or is it still unformed, undecided?

To me, this expresses our uniqueness, our inner being, what God knows of us but also what God loves in us. I often wonder whether the names we give to ourselves come close to the ones God might give to us.

What descriptive name could you give yourself right now? And what name would you love to receive from God? Here are some meanings of biblical names, as a starting point:

One helped by God – Azarel
Blessed – Baruch
Grace or favour – Hannah
Beloved of God – Jedidiah
Peace – Salome
Made happy by God – Mehetabel

Or are you looking for more negative names, such as Bitter – Mara? Perhaps you are quite content with the name you already have?

From desolation to delight
In this book, we are especially concerned with the journey from lost to found, the restoration of wholesome relationship with the one who loves us. Above, we read of a bereft woman speaking at a time when she saw her life as a journey from joy into sorrow – from Naomi to Mara. This difficult and painful journey from Pleasant to Bitter is one we know only too well. But as we read in the book of Ruth, she went on to find consolation in ways that she had not foreseen. Nobody could bring her husband and sons back, but her beloved daughter-in-law's baby brought a new joy. Perhaps by the end of her long life she was content to be

called Naomi again. Our lives, too, sometimes seem to descend into 'Mara' – bitterness and sorrow – but we do not know what is to come.

Isaiah 62:3, 4 describes a name change from lost to found which has meant a great deal to me personally. Jerusalem is depicted in the ancient image of the bride of God, who delights in her and lifts her up from her days of sorrow. Although the passage has a particular historical context, we are each free to identify ourselves with the holy city if it is an analogy that helps us:

> You shall be a crown of beauty in the hand of the Lord,
> and a royal diadem in the hand of your God.
> You shall no more be termed Forsaken [Azubah],
> and your land shall no more be termed Desolate
> [Shemamah];
> but you shall be called My Delight Is in Her
> [Hephzibah],
> and your land Married [Beulah];
> for the Lord delights in you,
> and your land shall be married.

Jerusalem, through her rebuilding after the exile, goes through a transformation from desolation to metaphorical marriage (here representing security and peace), discovering how much God delights in her. I believe very strongly that this renewal, so difficult to believe in from our places of brokenness and pain, is a gift offered to each of us by the Shepherd who calls us by name. For each of us, God has a name such as Hephzibah – 'My delight is in her.'

From lost to found: the journey to wholeness

In the next group of reflections, we will explore the ways we talk and think about ourselves. In each reflection, the journey from lost to found, of feeling broken to feeling whole, will be explored in a different way, but the essence will always be the shift from the statement 'I am lost' to the statement 'I am found'. Human voices from Scripture will express these feelings for us. The agent of that change will always be the Good Shepherd, expressed again through Scripture. It is God who transforms our brokenness, lifts us up and restores us to love.

Searching the Bible for words with which we can identify, we come to the book of Psalms. Here we find prayers which can speak for us and about us in our human condition, even up to 3000 years after some of them were first uttered. They contain many 'I am' statements, as the psalmist(s) struggled to understand themselves and their experiences in the light of God. Sometimes the psalms almost seem to be having a conversation with themselves, as a difficulty is raised, wrestled with and resolved in the light of faith. These ancient prayers can speak for us and help us as we, too, seek God's help in moving from pain to healing, distress to peace, lost to found.

Using the reflections

The structure of the reflections in this chapter is slightly different from those on relating to God and to the rest of the flock. The reflections are shorter but there are more of them. Rather than writing my own prayers to express a feeling, I have used words from the Psalms, and since the title of each speaks for itself, there is no need for an explanatory overview beyond a simple statement or question.

The reflections might be used in individual, private prayer and reflection or by a mutually supportive group. Sufficient time needs to be given to create a feeling of space around the Scripture and unhurried opportunity for meditating on the questions that are raised. The focus is on moving from negative to positive, from troubled to healthy feelings about 'self'.

Health warning

As with the earlier reflections, these are emotive issues, and difficult feelings may surface which leaders need to be ready to support and, if necessary, follow up with appropriate care. At the back of the book are suggestions for taking things further; this may include referral to an experienced listener such as a counsellor or trained pastoral minister. Taking part in reflections such as these may be the beginning of a long and much-needed journey of self-awareness for some, and bring up unhealed hurts for others, so it should only be undertaken with adequate forethought and pastoral care.

Suggestion for structuring a group session

I would suggest allowing at least half an hour to explore a reflection as a group. A deeper exploration might fill 50 minutes. Divide the time something like this:

- Begin with a prayer and/or a song and candle lighting.
- Present the title.
- Present the overview, for people to talk about with a neighbour as an ice breaker. Don't look for answers; just see what comes up. Allow up to five minutes.
- A member of the group reads the quotation from the Psalms, slowly and thoughtfully. Repeat two or three times, separated by pauses, as all listen.
- Pause for silent reflection for an agreed period of time – from two to ten or more minutes, depending on the group.
- The leader/other reads the comment, giving time and 'space' for any Scripture and questions.

- Talk with a partner or in a small group about issues that come up in the comment. Allow at least five minutes; 10-15 minutes might lead to deeper exploration, but don't get bogged down or sidetracked: this is only the start of the journey!
- Pause for calm, then read the second Psalm quotation in the same way as the first, with repetition and pauses, again allowing sufficient time for silent reflection.
- The leader/other reads the comment, followed by the questions.
- Groups or partners reflect on the questions. If there is more than one question, people may prefer to focus on one rather than rushing. Allow 10-15 minutes or more.
- If possible, read the closing prayer together, or one person reads for the whole group.
- Pause again, then close with an appropriate song or chant and blow out the candle.

Ten reflections about relating to self

1. From anxiety to awe

Overview

Thinking about how the Good Shepherd can move us from a state of worry that keeps us awake at night to a sense of wonder at God's work in our lives and creation.

Prayer of a lost sheep

You keep my eyelids from closing;
I am so troubled that I cannot speak.

Psalm 77:4

Comment

Jesus asks us, 'Can any of you by worrying add a single hour to your span of life?' (Luke 12:25). He says that worrying about material things is out of step with the life of faith – we should simply trust God and set our mind on the kingdom of heaven. Much as we might love this often-quoted 'lilies of the field' passage, it can be extremely difficult to follow his advice. We find ourselves talking back to him: 'Yes, but you don't know what the twenty-first century's like . . . you didn't have children . . . you never had to bother with credit ratings . . .'

Our 'Yes, but' has a hollowness about it. Deep down we know that part of the faith path is working out what living in trust and prioritising the kingdom means today. It is something that makes no sense in the eyes of the world; we can seem like fools for following our Shepherd. It is not a path of material security, but of spiritual security.

For reflection

- Who dares step out on such a way except one with a deep confidence in God?
- Whose life stories do you know of that resonate with this confidence?
- What kind of things disturb your peace and sense of trust?

Encountering the Shepherd

I will call to mind the deeds of the Lord;
I will remember your wonders of old.
I will meditate on all your work,
and muse on your mighty deeds.
Your way, O God, is holy.
What god is so great as our God?

Psalm 77:11-13

Comment

The psalmist starts Psalm 77 with great anxiety, yet by the end has moved to a much more positive frame of mind, simply by reflecting on God's works of wonder. For the psalmist, this will include the traditions already told among the people of Israel at the time, especially the liberation of the Hebrew slaves from Egypt and their journey through the wilderness to the Promised Land. It will also include the wonder of creation, which is a constantly unfolding marvel expressing the nature of God. Reflection on God's works brings the psalmist out of anxiety into a state of praise and acknowledgement of divine mystery and power.

For reflection

- Where do you see God's work in your personal history?
- How do you respond to God's work in creation?

Prayer of a found sheep

Oh my Shepherd, I am grateful that people so long ago felt moved to write about your presence in their lives, and that their words are still full of meaning and hope even now. It is amazing to me that I can pray the same prayer as somebody thousands of years ago, and that in all that time you have loved and held every soul that trusted in you – and those of us who struggle to trust, too. It helps me to accept that I, too, am held in your love, and that you hear my prayer.

I am grateful, too, for the daily revelations of your works all around me in creation: the changing seasons; the diversity of life; the beauty of human lives unfolding, from birth to youth, maturity to elderliness; the food we eat; the environments which sustain us. How amazing are your works, O God, and how I thank you.

Amen.

2. From humiliation to new life purpose

Overview

Thinking about how the Good Shepherd can move us from a feeling of demoralisation to a sense of fulfilment, meaning and purpose of a life lived for God.

Prayer of a lost sheep

I am a worm, and not human,
scorned by others, and despised by the people.

Psalm 22:6

Comment

If everyone in a workshop were asked to describe themselves as a creature expressing some quality they saw in themselves, we might feel a little concerned if someone described themselves as a worm. What creature(s) one chooses in such an exercise can be quite telling, although they vary depending on day-to-day circumstances. Popular quizzes on the subject reveal that lots of people like to identify themselves as wolves, bears, foxes, dolphins, eagles and so on, but there are not so many worms. (You might enjoy reflecting for a while on what creatures could represent your own traits.)

The truth is that God made us human beings and we have an innate dignity and worth because of that. To deny another their intrinsic worth is a dehumanising, degrading act – crucifixion was one such method of doing this, and was designed to cause the utmost humiliation as well as pain. Jesus was put through this violation of his humanity; indeed Psalm 22 has long been used by Christians to interpret what happened to him on the cross. But what does it mean to apply these words, 'I am a worm, and not human,' to Christ? What does it say to us in our own moments of humiliation, to know how low the powers of the world stooped to reduce him to this? How does it help us to know that our Shepherd went into that valley of shadows and death ahead of us, and emerged transformed?

For reflection
- How strongly is your sense of self-worth attached to the opinion others seem to have of you? Which opinions do you listen to?
- Whose opinions matter most to you?
- Who has the ability to crush your spirits or to lift them up?

Encountering the Shepherd
To him, indeed, shall all who sleep in the earth bow down;
before him shall bow all who go down to the dust,
and I shall live for him.   *Psalm 22:29*

Comment
Despite the apparent despair of the opening verses, the ending of Psalm 22 is full of hope in the future. The psalmist does not say 'I *am* living for God,' but talks in the future tense: 'I *shall* live for him.' This implies survival; it is a statement of belief in the continuation of life in a meaningful way. We might see this as a resurrection hope or a hope in physical healing and restoration – but it is a strong hope nevertheless.

The psalmist has shifted position. At the outset, it matters what other people think and their opinions can hurt – even physically, if they follow up their violent thoughts with actions. At the end, though, what matters is God: God, not public acclaim, is the driving force, the motivation for living. Defining ourselves by what we believe God sees in us and asks of us can be very different to defining ourselves by what reaction we receive from other people. Paul in Romans 8:31 says, 'If God is for us, who is against us?' The parable of the lost sheep reassures us that no matter what, the Shepherd is for us.

There is another shift, too. Likening himself to a worm, the psalmist is describing a state of humiliation, way down as low as you can go. Crawling on or under the earth is the lowliest of places to be, and being there is distressing. Down there, we know ourselves looked down on. But in verse 29, we find that the earth is the right and proper place for us to be: it is our nature; we are of the earth, like all life. This common bond of mortality is not humiliating but humbling. From this position, realising that we are all united in the gift of life, praise becomes possible.

For reflection
- What, to you, is the difference between humiliation and humility?

Prayer of a found sheep
Oh my Shepherd, it means so much that you already know what it is like to feel demoralised, despised, humiliated, treated with contempt. How much you suffered helps me to see my own life from a different perspective, as it does to know that you understand me and care about me. You come to me down at ground level; you don't mind stooping and getting yourself dirty in order to reach me. Lift me up so that I can feel glad of your presence, glad of life itself. Help me to put you at the heart of my life, to see you as the meaning and the love behind everything.

Amen.

3. From sorrow to strength

Overview

Thinking about how the Good Shepherd can help us in our journey through grief to find consolation in God.

Prayer of a lost sheep

Be gracious to me, O Lord, for I am in distress;
my eye wastes away from grief,
my soul and body also.   *Psalm 31:9*

Comment

Part of living means hurting, simply because of the inevitable separations, endings and deaths we endure. When that deep sadness seeps into every niche of our being, it is as though our own soul has died and our whole identity is taken up with this feeling: 'I am sadness itself. I am sorrow.'

Grief both unites us as a universal experience and isolates us: nobody can ever fully understand our personal experience; neither can we fully articulate it. From this troubled place, the psalmist asks for God's graciousness. God alone, who sees the heart, fully understands our broken-heartedness. Such brokenness takes time to heal, and it is God who has the patience to hold us throughout that time. This is the valley of the shadow of death, which the Shepherd guides us through.

Another psalm which makes the same request, 'Be gracious to me, O God' (56:1), also gives us the beautiful image of God putting our tears into a bottle (verse 8), to preserve them. God notices our tears, our pain. It is a sign of love.

For reflection
- How has the experience of loss shaped you?
- How has it affected the way you relate to others and to God?

Encountering the Shepherd

Be strong, and let your heart take courage,
all you who wait for the Lord.   *Psalm 31:24*

This call to be strong comes from a human being thousands of years ago who, like us, lived through heartbreak and knew the courage it demands. Simply by enduring these times, we grow emotionally and spiritually and become a strength to others.

To me, the patience God shows, holding us in love for as long as it takes, is reflected back in our own patience with others. For we do not have the fullness of God in the here and now; we live in hope. We wait with longing. We wait for that promised sense of presence which we know will heal all. That hope, I think, is part of what helps us to hold on through difficult times, like the shelter we see in the distance on a long and difficult journey. God is our refuge, as Psalm 31 says, but God will be more than that – the destination of our journey, our true home. 'I shall dwell in the house of the Lord my whole life long,' says the closing verse of Psalm 23. This is where the Shepherd is leading us – to a place where there is no more grief, only joy.

For reflection
- What experiences in your life have led you to develop greater courage and endurance?
- What is your future longing?
- How do you picture that divine dwelling?

Prayer of a found sheep

Oh my Shepherd, nothing prepared me for this. I am simply grateful for your words of reassurance, that you are with me 'even though I walk through the darkest valley'. I need say nothing to you for you understand my heart. I can sit quietly with you, I can weep with you, I can sleep in your presence, safe despite the pain. Bring me through this difficult time; protect me while I am so vulnerable, while my feelings are so raw. My companion through sorrow and in joy, lead me to deeper wisdom so that I may grow and be a strength to others who pass this way, and despite the pain, let me never stop loving, or choosing life in abundance.

Amen.

4. From guilt to gratitude

Overview

Thinking about how the Good Shepherd can help us lay down our burdens of guilt, to find new freedom through God's blessing.

Prayer of a lost sheep

For I am ready to fall,
and my pain is ever with me.
I confess my iniquity;
I am sorry for my sin.

Psalm 38:17, 18

Comment

I am sorry. I am *sorry*. Feeling guilty absorbs a great deal of emotional energy. Talking about it can help, if we can find the right person to talk to. The Shepherd is always the right 'person'. Even if we can think of nobody we wish to confide in, we can utter our most intimate thoughts to God who already knows. Until we do this, our identity can become bound up with the remorse we are carrying round; it enslaves us. This is because we care. If we didn't care about the consequences of our thoughts, actions and words, then we would not suffer agonies of guilt. If we did not look deeply into our lives and the effect we have on other living things, we would have no remorse, no shame.

Jesus our Shepherd walked the earth freeing people from their sense of guilt. Those healing words, 'Your sins are forgiven,' were words of unbinding, of freedom. They are medicine to the soul. They are spoken to us, lost sheep that we are.

For reflection
- How do you, or how can you, bring troubled feelings and burdens to God in prayer?

Encountering the Shepherd
But I am like a green olive tree
in the house of God.
I trust in the steadfast love of God
for ever and ever.
I will thank you for ever,
because of what you have done.
In the presence of the faithful
I will proclaim your name, for it is good.

Psalm 52:8, 9

Comment
The person praying 'I am ready to fall; I am sorry for my sin', is a broken person. Compare this state of distress with the luscious image above: 'I am like a green olive tree in the house of God.' I am like a flourishing, verdant, fruit-bearing

tree in a holy place, well tended and much appreciated. I am beautiful and wholesome. What can shift us from the first 'I am' to the second, from the sickness of guilt to the wholeness of the olive tree?

I think a clue lies in verse 8, the reference to God's steadfast love, and in verse 9: 'I will thank you for ever, because of what you have done.' What is it, this mighty and lovely act, that makes the psalmist so glad? What is it that draws out our gratitude and our joy? Perhaps we each have our own answers, relating to God's presence in our own lives, but the gift of grace – God's desire to forgive us, to set us free – is crucial to our faith. We are not called to live in misery because of what we have done, but to step into the new life God offers us, no longer trusting in our own righteousness but in God's mercy.

For reflection
- When you are troubled, what allows you to let go of feelings of remorse?
- What is it that you wish to thank God for, for evermore?

Prayer of a found sheep
Oh my Shepherd, thank you for giving me freedom. Let me accept your gift so that I can feel lighter, happier, more able to follow you gladly. Let the weight of worry fall away. Let me look back on my past with wisdom, O God, to understand myself and have compassion on myself, and let me learn from my experiences. Let me be a wiser, humbler, more loving and kindly person now, less quick to judge others. Let this change me for good, so that I can grow in your grace and goodness and be at peace with myself.

Amen.

5. From fear to trust

Overview

Thinking about how the Good Shepherd can help us move out of fearfulness towards a greater sense of peace.

Prayer of a lost sheep

My enemies trample on me all day long,
for many fight against me.
O Most High, when I am afraid,
I put my trust in you.   *Psalm 56:2, 3*

Comment

The psalmist describes a situation of conflict; there are adversaries, people setting themselves in opposition, acting to undermine and even to destroy. Sometimes we cope well with antagonistic situations and get a buzz out of conflict, especially if we win. But this person already feels beaten. Confidence is broken and fear takes hold.

Our everyday lives sometimes present us with situations where we feel like this. Panic attacks or other stress-related reactions can start to bother us because fear is not just an emotion; it is a physical response too. 'I am stressed', or 'I get anxious easily', can become part of our identity. We can use it to explain to others why we are behaving in a certain way or avoiding certain people or situations. But what is it that is making us feel so threatened? Who or what can help us deal with these issues in a practical as well as a spiritual way?

For reflection

- Although afraid, the psalmist knows what to do: 'O Most High, when I am afraid, I put my trust in you.' What does this mean to you? What does it involve *doing*?

183

Encountering the Shepherd
In God, whose word I praise,
in the Lord, whose word I praise,
in God I trust; I am not afraid.
What can a mere mortal do to me?

Psalm 56:10, 11

Comment
Psalm 56 develops this idea of trust. It seems that the prayer shifts from lost to found. In verse 11, the emphasis has changed from 'I am afraid so I trust' to 'I trust; I am not afraid.' The second position seems the more confident one.

What moves the psalmist out of fear into trust? What inspires the words of praise? We find out if we read to the end of the psalm: 'You have delivered my soul from death, and my feet from falling, so that I may walk before God in the light of life' (verse 13).

Deliverance from death, saving feet from slipping, walking before God . . . these sound like journeying or shepherding images: they are the protective actions of a shepherd, armed with rod and staff.

For reflection
- What is it that causes you fear? Is it mere mortals, or something else?
- What does walking 'in the light of life' mean to you?

Prayer of a found sheep
Oh my Shepherd, thank you for helping me to move out of fear and into trust. Thank you that even though things are uncertain, I know that if I must walk the way that has been worrying me, then I will walk it with you, and with you my soul is safe. Help me to be ever mindful of your presence,

your rod and staff comforting me as I walk a difficult path. Let me gain wisdom and strength from this experience, and joy as I discover new depth to our love and the simplicity of trusting in you.

Amen.

6. From frustration to gladness

Overview

Thinking about how the Good Shepherd can lead us on from our feelings of exasperation and that we alone are trying to make a positive difference, to a sense of appreciation for God's infinite goodness.

Prayer of a lost sheep

Too long have I had my dwelling
among those who hate peace.
I am for peace;
but when I speak,
they are for war.   *Psalm 120:6, 7*

Comment

The feeling that we alone are holding out for goodness and truth can be a terribly lonely experience. We see people in the world, and read of saints who went before us, in extremes of this very position. Part of what makes them remarkable is their capacity to hold out. We might find ourselves wondering whether we would have the courage to do the same. Yet sometimes it is the situation itself that challenges us to find a strength we never knew we had, to stand up and speak out, because it is that one particular issue we find we cannot keep silent about. Here, I think, lie seeds of love-inspired courage.

185

The less positive side is that we can sometimes become entrenched in a position which we are defending so strongly it can be difficult to understand the other standpoint and discuss peace terms. It sounds as though the psalmist has reached this difficult position, where negotiations break down. He (or she) is blaming the others and asserting innocence. But even a position of rightness and a desire for peace can be spoken of in ways that make conversation difficult.

For reflection
- Who inspires you in the way they have stood up for peace?
- How does this issue relate to your own experience?
- What kind of peace is it that you really want? How do you bring this desire into your prayers?

Encountering the Shepherd
The Lord is my strength and my shield;
in him my heart trusts;
so I am helped, and my heart exults,
and with my song I give thanks to him.

Psalm 28:7

Comment
'I am helped, and my heart exults', the psalmist sings. The journey from feeling we have to 'fight for peace', so to speak, by our own efforts, to a sense of divine help, is where we find some of the peace that we need. True peace is of God; our human limitation makes it very difficult for us to achieve complete harmony amongst ourselves without that holy spirit of reconciliation, compassion, gentleness and love. All the qualities we need to live together in peace come

from God; they are fruits of God's Spirit working in us: 'love, joy, peace, patience, kindness, generosity, faithfulness, gentleness, and self-control' (Galatians 5:22, 23). We might wish to add other qualities to the list, too, such as honesty, humility and simplicity.

God working in us works miracles of transformation. It does not mean our lives are trouble free, but it means we respond to troubles from a peaceful heart. I think this is a huge part of what the spiritual journey is about, but it is not something we learn easily or quickly. Inner peace comes with time, as a gift from God. Even glimmers of it lift our hearts; they are moments of gladness when suddenly we feel safe, or we feel supported, despite our situation. Such experiences give substance to our life of faith; they are a help from God.

For reflection
- What spiritual qualities would you add to the list Paul gives us in Galatians 5:22, 23?
- When have you felt a sense of receiving genuine help in your life? How did it make you feel?

Prayer of a found sheep
When you reach out to me, my Shepherd, all troubles seem to fall away. For that precious moment I can live wholly in your embrace and be strengthened, affirmed, understood. I see my desperate attempts to fight my corner from a different perspective; I find new words, a new heart, my hope is renewed. Thank you, O God, for working in my life, guiding me to become a deeper, gentler person, more able to live out your kingdom values in the world, with not just words but works of true peace.

Amen.

7. From loneliness to comfort

Overview

Thinking about how the Good Shepherd can draw us out of our feelings of isolation, towards a sense of being held always in God's loving presence.

Prayer of a lost sheep

Turn to me and be gracious to me,
for I am lonely and afflicted.
Relieve the troubles of my heart,
and bring me out of my distress.

Psalm 25:16, 17

Comment

The times I have dared to utter these words, 'I am lonely', I have also often found myself in tears. Admitting our loneliness seems to open a floodgate; it is an admission that we are not giving and receiving the love we need. There is an emptiness, a meaninglessness and joylessness in our lives, even a sense of failure.

People of faith are sometimes led to believe that they are not allowed to feel like this: 'rejoice always', we hear (1 Thessalonians 5:16). But it is not as simple as that. Loneliness is not just about being physically alone. We can live in solitude without feeling lonely, and we can be surrounded by people yet feel isolated, ignored, misunderstood and insignificant. This can happen in a church, in a marriage, in a workplace . . . and often without others realising.

The psalmist reminds us that we need to bring this loneliness to God in prayer. If we do not, then we risk the loneliness eating away at our self-image so we will find ourselves identifying as a lonely soul. God wants us to love and be loved, and God will work on our loneliness if we ask, but not necessarily in ways that we expect.

For reflection
- What does loneliness mean to you?
- In times of loneliness, what have you longed for most?

Encountering the Shepherd

How weighty to me are your thoughts, O God!
How vast is the sum of them!
I try to count them – they are more than the sand;
I wake – I am still with you.   *Psalm 139:17, 18*

Comment

Psalm 139 reassures us of the presence of God. The discovery, 'I am still with you', can help us see ourselves differently. Rather than identifying mainly with an unhappy social situation, we start to identify more as God's beloved. God loves us and never leaves us.

This sounds wonderful, but I know from experience that it can be difficult to believe: what good is a God who cannot physically hold us, anyway? The answer to that pain-loaded question comes with time – God's time. Our faith tells us that however lonely we feel, we are not alone. There is mystery in this and trust, but there is also a path to comfort: the Shepherd's love is not the same as that of the rest of the flock – it is deeper and greater by far.

For reflection
- Have there ever been experiences in your life which have touched you somehow with a sense of deep love?
- What does the love of God mean to you?

Prayer of a found sheep

Thank you, my Shepherd, that you have touched me with your presence, and that I know that you are with me, walking alongside me. Help me to recognise the times when you and I walk alone together as precious in their own way, times to listen to you, share with you, draw closer in love. I know you want me to love and be loved by others, and I trust you to guide me on into new situations where this can happen. Prepare me for happier relationships, O God; free me from my resentments and hurts so that I can relax in others' company. Help me to turn to you first for my needs, my Shepherd, for you are my comfort.

Amen.

8. From lost to loved

Overview

Thinking about how the Good Shepherd can find us and restore us to the deep love that God has for us.

Prayer of a lost sheep

I have gone astray like a lost sheep;
seek out your servant,
for I do not forget your commandments.

Psalm 119:176

Comment

This prayer epitomises the concern of this book: the sense of lostness when we feel far from God and our faith community. The psalmist helps us to recognise our situation and name it – and this is an important step in accepting the help of the Shepherd when it comes. Identifying ourselves as lost or straying can require a good deal of honesty and integrity from us – there is often pressure on Christians to appear perfect, yet this is impossible.

Feelings of lostness can come and go – for some it is a longer-lasting state than others, yet God does not give up on anybody. Our low days, or low years, are known and held; our Shepherd is well aware of our straying and is already on our tracks, already close by, helping us in ways we cannot see or appreciate. This is our hope; it is what our faith gives us as a promise of grace to hold on to when life is difficult.

The last words of the prayer above invite us to reflect on what the way of the Shepherd really is. What is or what are God's commandments? Jesus singled out two from the Hebrew Scriptures – that we are to love God with our whole heart, mind and being, and our neighbour as ourself. Then, in John's Gospel, his command is given that we love one another. Remembering these three laws of love is remembering the love we know we need and want at the heart of our being. When we ask for love, I think God gives it to us, but not necessarily how we might expect. To know we are loved by God is to know we are not lost.

For reflection

- What does it mean to you to be lost or astray?
- How do you respond to God's commands of love?

Encountering the Shepherd

My beloved is mine and I am his;
he pastures his flock among the lilies.

Song of Songs 2:16

Comment

This verse (not from the Psalms this time) gives us a different way of reflecting on the Shepherd that allows us to identify as a human being rather than a sheep for a change! The lover or bridegroom in the Song of Songs is a shepherd, and he has a beautiful place to lead his flock, down by the stream where the lilies grow. The green pastures and restful waters of Psalm 23 spring to mind. A beautiful young woman speaks of her lover with words of mystical depth. This is not simply an erotic insert into the Scriptures; the images of intimate love offer us a way of talking about the soul's relationship with the divine: 'my beloved is mine and I am his.'

As a statement of identity, this feeling of oneness, of belonging to and with God, can hardly be paralleled. In the soul's union with the divine, faith tells us we find our deepest bliss and the true meaning and purpose of our lives. How can we reach this paradise, from our positions of confusion and lostness? Well, it is God's will. God yearns for us, and this is the strongest reassurance that it will happen – but only when we are ready.

Prayer of a found sheep

My Shepherd, my Beloved, you set my heart on fire with love for you. Everything seems brighter and more hopeful in those moments when I sense your living presence knowing and cherishing me. Let me know your love more deeply, until I am filled with longing to be yours, deeply and for always, no longer lost but found because I belong with you.

Amen.

9. From need to sufficiency

Overview

Thinking about how the Good Shepherd can move us on from our feelings of neediness to a sense of complete confidence in God.

Prayer of a lost sheep

But I am poor and needy;
hasten to me, O God!
You are my help and my deliverer;
O Lord, do not delay!   *Psalm 70:5*

Comment

If the statement of identity were just 'I am poor,' we could be St Francis, or one of the disciples even, because they embraced poverty joyfully and found a way of living simply in which they found God. As we know, people still do this – it can be a spiritual calling. But poverty, unless chosen for ascetic reasons, tends to go hand in hand with anxiety, poor diet and health, and reduced opportunities to engage fully in life. It can be an emotional, educational and spiritual impoverishment as well as material. This, I am sure, is not 'of God'.

The psalmist does not just say 'I am poor', but also 'I am needy.' This neediness qualifies the poverty – it indicates a state of unhappiness. Recognising our needs can help us to meet them. The psalmist shows us the best thing to do with these needs: take them to God in prayer.

For reflection

- Have you ever experienced poverty, materially, emotionally or spiritually?
- What did Jesus mean when he said 'blessed are the poor in spirit' (Matthew 5:3)?
- What are your genuine *needs*, as distinct from the things you *want*?

Encountering the Shepherd

Nevertheless I am continually with you;
you hold my right hand.

You guide me with your counsel,
and afterwards you will receive me with honour.
Whom have I in heaven but you?
And there is nothing on earth that I desire other than you.

Psalm 73:23-25

Comment

'I am continually with you.' What a firm and confident statement of identity to make to God. 'You hold my right hand . . . you guide me.' Where does such faith come from, if not from personal experience of God's presence?

How do we reach this level of confidence in God? The image of the good shepherd seems to offer us just that confidence – the one who is always with us, guiding us for our own good. If we stay with the imagery of the previous reflection and think of our soul as the Shepherd's beloved, then we find our hand is held too, firmly, warmly, safely. But can we affirm that this presence is continual? Although I *believe* I am with God all the time, I am not fully mindful all the while. I forget, I get preoccupied, I wander off. On the great day when I can be *continuously* aware of that divine love, then I will not be lost any more. This gives me something to aspire to; it is an image of paradise. I think God draws us all to that awareness in the journey of our lives.

While we dwell on our lack, our need, our poverty, it absorbs our thoughts. The psalmist offers a challenge to this preoccupation with need: 'there is nothing on earth that I desire other than you.' This is the statement of a lover, not a beggar; it shows a soul whose true longing is not for material wealth but for God. We read of such longing in the Gospels – Jesus said, 'where your treasure is, there your heart will be also' (Matthew 6:21). How are we to understand this, faced with our own needs and the poverty we see in the world around us?

For reflection
- How do we really come to love God so much that we can say 'there is nothing on earth that I desire other than you'?
- What is it that helps you to stay mindful of God's presence?

Prayer of a found sheep
My beloved Shepherd, all I want is to follow you, to be with you, to hear your voice, to see your face. Help me to dwell on you more constantly, to let the distractions diminish, the doubts cease, the hankering after anything but you, die away. Wrapped up in your love, let me surrender my burdens, trusting at last that you know my needs and meet them, simply, easily, naturally. You hold me, the whole of me, all that I was, all that I will be, and you love me. This is all I need to know for my life to be touched with joy.

Amen.

10. From sickness to salvation

Overview
Thinking about how the Good Shepherd knows our hurts and can bathe us in love, for our soul's renewal.

Prayer of a lost sheep
Be gracious to me, O Lord, for I am languishing;
O Lord, heal me, for my bones are shaking with terror.

Psalm 6:2

Comment

The psalmist is struggling with serious sickness, which in turn is causing fear and sleeplessness. He feels that others are contemptuous, perhaps believing God to be behind this suffering. 'I am languishing' is a strongly negative statement to make – the word 'languishing' conveys a loss of strength, a state of hopelessness, a prison-like situation in which a person has little power to help themselves and has become dispirited.

In this state of disempowerment, our problems can easily become magnified, our frame of mind depressed. The healing the psalmist cries out for needs to be not just a physical healing but also a healing of spirit, of mental strength to endure and live in hope.

For reflection

- What frightens you?
- Have you ever felt as though you were languishing? If so, what helped you?

Encountering the Shepherd

I am yours; save me.

Psalm 119:94

Comment

This is one of the shortest prayers in the Bible, and one of my favourites. It opens with a statement of identity which is true for all of us, and which, if we can believe it, has transforming power in our lives: 'I am yours' or 'I belong to God'. Because we belong to God, the petition 'save me' is already answered. We are safe. God is not a great ogre to go running from, but the one who loves us, the one to whom we belong. The love God has for us is our promise of safety.

The parable of the lost sheep illustrates this reassuring truth, that however far we stray, wherever we hide, whatever the danger in which we find ourselves, the Shepherd knows and lifts us up. The Shepherd is the lover of our souls, ready to lay down his life for us, and we are safe.

For reflection
- What does it mean to be safe?
- What does it mean to belong to God?
- What experiences have you had of suddenly feeling very safe? Are these experiences associated with particular people or places?

Prayer of a found sheep
Oh my Shepherd, thank you for taking away the feelings of fear and despair that made me want to run away and hide from you. Thank you for coming to find me and lift me up, and for restoring my soul to health. I am grateful that I have you, that I am yours, and I wish to follow you more truly and to know you more deeply. I am grateful that in you I feel safe to face life and even death, and to live in hope of resurrection joy. In this moment, I am grateful that I can simply sit in your presence and feel at peace, knowing that you love me perfectly and for ever.

Amen.

Moving on

However difficult our terrain, however far we feel we have strayed, we are safe because God knows where we are. In fact, God is always there with us, closer than we realise – our constant, loving and wise companion. Something stops us believing this sometimes, because the path seems too difficult: surely we have got lost. And there are times when we try to run away from that presence, forgetting that it is Love itself, all-forgiving, all-compassionate, all-merciful. But we can no more hide from God than we can refuse to breathe. In God 'we live and move and have our being' (Acts 17:28).

With this in mind, we have thought especially about John 10:1-16, where Jesus says, 'I am the good shepherd.' The metaphor has helped us to explore what it can mean to feel lost and what it can mean to feel found and loved by God.

There are seven 'I am' statements in John's Gospel, and they invite us to associate Jesus with the revelation of God to Moses:

> God said to Moses, 'I am who I am.' He said further, 'Thus you shall say to the Israelites, "I am has sent me to you."' *Exodus 3:14*

As well as 'I am the good shepherd,' according to the Gospel of John Jesus also says:

- I am the bread of life (John 6:35, 48).
- I am the light of the world (John 8:12; 9:5).
- I am the door or the gateway of the sheepfold (John 10:9).
- I am the resurrection and the life (John 11:25).

- I am the way, and the truth, and the life (John 14:6).
- I am the true vine (John 15:1).

This mystical, figurative language begs us to ask, and to keep asking, 'What does this *mean*?' Over the centuries, these words have meant so many things to so many people – each time a fresh revelation of insight into the nature of Christ. They seem, in a way, to anticipate the question of St Francis of Assisi, which we reflected on earlier. Inspired by him, we can ask in prayer, 'Who are you, O God, and who am I?' And then, 'If you are the Shepherd, then who am I?' As we move on, extending the message of the Good Shepherd into our wider life, we can ask the same question in different ways:

- If you are the bread, then what am I?
- If you are the light, what am I?
- If you are the door to the sheepfold, what am I?

We can ask the same question of all the other images the Scriptures give us of God: a green pasture, a mother bird, a shield, the sun, and so on:

- Who and what are we, in relation to God and to the rest of humanity, and the whole of creation?

Our answers to these questions change over the years; truth has unfathomable depth, but it also has a simplicity to it. Somewhere in our searching, we are touched by the paradox that we are both nothing and 'a little lower than angels' (Psalm 8). We are but dust, and to dust we will return, but we are also the house of God, children of the light. We have no reason for self-glory, but we have every reason to glory in God.

Unconditional love is not *all* the Bible talks about, by any means, and without a guide, we can struggle to navigate its pages as with a map. But who better to guide us through our Scriptures and through life itself than the Shepherd? Who better to act as our interpreter, or the lens through which we read? What better to search for than the footprints of the shepherd, picking out a path for us to follow? And who better to listen for, when we find ourselves in unfamiliar territory, unsure which way to go? With the Shepherd at home in our hearts, how can we ever be lost? In this loving presence, our souls are restored.

Postscript: Go safely

Whole books have been written on many of the individual themes I have brought together in *Rejoice with Me*. Having touched briefly on a range of thoughts and feelings by reading this book, you might find yourself identifying areas which you want to explore in more detail.

If you do feel moved to take some of the issues you have thought about further, here are some avenues open to you:

- Search online through the publications available and see if anything leaps out at you – or visit a good bookshop.
- Talk to others who seem to have worked through such issues themselves and ask them if they can recommend books, courses, retreats or groups, but remember that their path is not your path – you don't have to follow in their footsteps.
- Consider counselling. Although counselling is not normally faith based, it is rooted in deeply humanitarian principles of empathy and respect, and a qualified counsellor will be supportive of your faith perspective.
- Consider visiting a spiritual director or accompanier (a wise and non-judgemental Christian with life experience and good listening skills) to talk about your faith journey. Think about following a programme of study, perhaps a

Bible study course or a series of lectures, that will help you gain new perspectives on reading Scripture. Keep a journal of your thoughts and feelings, with a focus on noticing encounters with the Good Shepherd in your life, to encourage you.

• Consider moving on from your current situation if it is causing a barrier to love, or consider, as a first step, raising the issues with those concerned to see if they can be resolved.

• Remind yourself that there is a huge variety of Christian groups. Every church worships in a slightly different way, with a slightly different collective attitude and outlook. By searching, you are quite likely, in time, to find somewhere that contributes to your sense of well-being rather than diminishing it.

• Be open to things that come up naturally which seem to be meaningful. God, as they say, works in mysterious ways.

• Pray more, for longer, talking to God honestly about your feelings and also allowing plenty of time to listen and to just sit quietly in God's loving presence, alone or within a group.

A closing prayer

May God our Shepherd guide you and keep you,
and may you walk with courage,
whether the path be rough or smooth,
knowing yourself loved no matter what,
throughout your days.
Amen.

Also by Annie Heppenstall

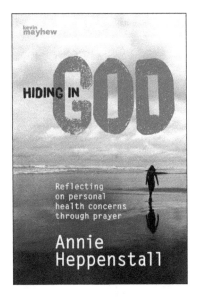

Hiding in God
1501341

www.kevinmayhew.com